Nita Mehta's
Dilli ka Khaana

Nita Mehta's
Dilli ka Khaana

100% TRIED & TESTED RECIPES

Nita Mehta
B.Sc. (Home Science), M.Sc. (Food and Nutrition) Gold Medalist

Tanya Mehta

SNAB
Publishers Pvt. Ltd.

Reprint 2008

ISBN 978-81-7869-078-0

Food Styling & Photography: **SNAB** 🌐

Layout and laser typesetting:

National Information
Technology Academy
3A/3, Asaf Ali Road
New Delhi-110002
☎ 23252948

Published by:

SNAB 🌐
Publishers Pvt Ltd
3A/3 Asaf Ali Road
New   Delhi-110002
Tel:23250091, 23252948
Telefax:.91-11-23250091

Editorial and Marketing office:
E-159, Greater Kailash-II, N.Delhi-110048
Tel: 91-11-29214011, 29218727, 29218574
Fax: 91-11-29225218, 29229558
E-Mail: nitamehta@email.com
nitamehta@nitamehta.com

The Best of Cookery Books *Website:* http://www.nitamehta.com
Website: http://www.snabindia.com

Printed at:
BRIJBASI ART PRESS LTD.

Distributed by:
THE VARIETY BOOK DEPOT
A.V.G. Bhavan, M 3 Con Circus
New Delhi - 110 001
Tel: 23417175, 23412567; Fax: 23415335
E-mail: varietybookdepot@rediffmail.com

Price: Rs. 195/-

Picture on cover:	Aloo ki Tikki
	Bervi Poori aur Aloo Chhole
Picture on page 1:	Fruit Kulle, Kathi Roti
Picture on page 2-3:	Sabut Simla Mirch, Murg Changezi
	Varqi Parantha
Picture on page 4:	Vegetable Korma, Dal Makhani
Picture on page 94:	Moong Chillah with Hari Chutney
	Matar Kachouri aur Subzi

Contributing Writers :
Anurag Mehta
Subhash Mehta

Editorial & Proofreading :
Rakesh
Rajesh

Introduction

What exactly is Delhi food? To find out, we took a walk around the old city & got the feel of the food eaten in *Purani Dilli*. The food was rich & varied. Delhi has a very colourful history and has had many different influences on the cuisine and culture of the people. There is such a variety and combination of rich Punjabi food, tasty vegetarian food of Uttar Pradesh and delicious non veg Mughlai khaana.

Roaming around the streets of *Chandni Chowk, the Jama Masjid areas and Daryaganj,* we thoroughly enjoyed the street foods. I spoke to food-stall owners, the expert cooks in their own specialties, asked them to share their secrets of masalas and other cooking ingredients. We tried out all the recipes and I have penned down these to give you the real, authentic Delhi food!

The book starts with a section on Chaats which is followed by Nashta or Snacks. The extremely soft *dahi badas of Chandni Chowk,* with just the right crispness, are dificult to get anywhere else. I admire and marvel at the perseverance of these dedicated Dilli chaat waalahs, who get shoulder aches while beating the ground dal for a long stretch of time. However, keeping in mind the busy life style of today, I have made the task much simpler by adding a pinch of baking powder and using an electric hand mixer for beating purposes. The delicious *Fruit Kulle* available at *Nai Sarak at Sultan's shop* are a specialty of Delhi. *Karim* of old Delhi is popular all over India with the people who are really *shokeen* (fond of) of non veg kebabs and also proper non veg meal dishes. And what better brunch can one have on a Sunday than the *Bervi Poori with Aloo ki Subzi from the famous Kedarnath Premchand Halwai of Chandni Chowk.*

For the grand finale we have the desi ghee ki *jalebi of Dariba.* Top it with rabri for a divine taste! The real malaidar kulfi frozen in a mixture of salt and ice and served on sticks is a treat. I have not used the same freezing mixture of ice and salt which freezes the kulfis in minutes as it is not too practical in home cooking. All the recipes are modified and made simple to cook and serve, retaining the authenticity of the food. As always, all the recipes are thoroughly tried and tested. So get ready to win the hearts as "The way to your man's heart is through Dilli ka Khaana".

Nita Mehta

Contents

Chandni Chowk Ki
CHAAT

Ram Laddoo

Topped with Mooli & Hari Chutney

A very common street food in the lanes of old Delhi. While roaming in chandini chowk, I once happened to ask a hawker selling these laddoos. "How do you make your laddoos so light and fluffy" I was rather upset with his reply."You know memsahib (mam), my arm and shoulder start paining when I beat the pithi (ground dal) for more than 30 minutes everyday"

At that moment I actually felt like gifting him an electric hand mixer to make his job simpler.Thanks to the modern machines. The same lightness can now be achieved by beating the ground dal with an electric mixture for about 5-7 minutes and without giving us any aches and pains!

Picture on cover   *Serves 5-6*

½ cup (200 gm) dhuli mung ki dal (husked green beans)
½ cup channe ki dal
½ tsp salt, oil for deep frying

ACCOMPANIMENTS
1 mooli (white radish) - peeled and grated, some hari chutney

1. Wash both the dals and soak together in some water overnight.
2. Next day strain dals. Grind them together to a **rough** paste in a mixer grinder, using very little water, only if required. Do not make it into a smooth paste.
3. Beat ground dal in a bowl with an electric hand mixer for 5-7 minutes till it feels really light and frothy of a soft dropping consistency, like that of a cake batter. Add salt. Mix well. To check if it is done put a small ball of beaten dal paste in a bowl of water. If it rises to the surface, it is done, otherwise beat some more.
4. Heat oil in a kadhai for deep frying. To test if oil is hot enough, drop a little paste into the kadhai. It should rise to the surface almost immediately.
5. Using wet fingers drop small amounts of paste into oil. Reduce heat to medium. When bubbles appear on the surface, turn and fry till golden yellow. Drain on paper napkins and serve topped with grated mooli and hari chutney.

Fruit Kulle

Hollowed cups of charcoal roasted potatoes are sold at Nai Sarak at the shop of Sultan. However, the potatoes can be boiled for a more practical version for the home kitchen. It started with potatoes and now kullas of all kinds of fruit and vegetable have become popular.

Serves 6   *Picture on page 1*

3 small potatoes - boiled
3 small tomatoes
1 kheera - peeled and cut into 6 pieces, about 1½" long

FILLING
½ cup channas (safeed chhole) - soak in warm water for 1 hour
½ cup fresh anaar ke dane (pomegranate kernels)
½ cup grapes (use black or green) - each cut into half from the middle
½ cup peas (matar)- boiled
2-3 green chillies - deseeded and chopped
1-2 tbsp chaat masala, preferably kala chat masala
½ tsp bhuna jeera (roasted cumin powder)
juice of ½ lemon
salt to taste

1. Drain channas. Put them in a pressure cooker with 1 tsp salt and 1 cup water. Pressure cook to give 1 whistle. Remove from fire. Strain the channas after the pressure drops. Leave them in the strainer (channi) for all the water to drain out.

2. Peel the boiled potatoes. Cut each potato into 2 halves. Scoop out each piece with the help of a scooper or knife to get hollow cups. Sprinkle some lemon juice and chat masala in the potato cups and rub well. Keep aside.

3. Cut the tomato into halves and scoop out the filling. Similarly scoop out the cucumber pieces with a knife or scooper, keeping the base intact. Sprinkle some lemon juice and chat masala in the cups.

4. For the filling, mix all ingredients in a bowl. Check the filling and make it to your taste. Keep aside.

5. Fill each hollowed vegetable with this filling, heaping it a little. Serve.

 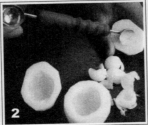 

Aloo ki Tikki

Picture on cover   *Serves 8*

5 medium (600 gm) potatoes - boiled and mashed
2 tbsp cornflour
1 tsp salt, ½ tsp baking powder
5-6 tbsp ghee or oil for shallow frying

FILLING
½ cup dhuli moong dal (split, skinned green beans)
½ tsp jeera (cumin seed), 2 pinches hing (asafoetida)
½" piece ginger - finely chopped, 1 green chilli - finely chopped
1 tsp dhania powder, ½ tsp red chilli powder
½ tsp chaat masala, ½ tsp garam masala
1 tbsp coriander leaves - chopped, ½ tsp salt

ACCOMPANIMENT
meethi imli chutney or saunth, page 91

1. For the filling, soak dal overnight or for at least for 3-4 hours in water, keeping the water 2" above the dal. Drain dal and grind in a mixer to a rough paste. Do not grind too much, you should be able to see some whole dal grains in the dal paste. Grind for a few seconds only. Push down the dal on the sides of the mixer with a spatula or knife and grind again for a few seconds to a rough paste.

2. For the filling, heat 3 tbsp oil or ghee in a kadhai. Add jeera and hing. Let jeera turn golden. Remove from fire. Add ginger, chopped green chilli, dhania powder, red chillies, chat masala and garam masala. Return to fire. Add coriander and dal paste. Add salt. Stir continuously for about 5 minutes on low medium heat. Do not dry it too much. Remove from fire and keep aside to cool.

3. Boil, peel and grate potatoes. Sprinkle 2 tbsp cornflour, 1 tsp salt and baking powder on the potatoes. Mix nicely so that the ingredients mix together.

4. Divide the potato mixture into 8 portions. Take a ball of mashed potatoes. Make a shallow cup with the ball of mashed potatoes. Place a tbsp full of dal filling in centre and seal well from all sides to cover the filling.

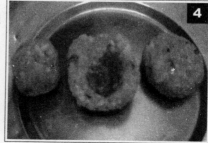

5. Heat oil on a non stick tawa or a frying pan. Shallow fry 2-3 tikkis at a time on low medium heat till golden and crisp on both sides. Once done, shift to the sides and put fresh ones in the centre. This way the tikkis turn really crisp. Serve hot topped with lots of imli ki meethi chutney.

Moong Chillah
with Hari Chutney

Lentil pancakes topped with onion, tomato and paneer, served folded into ____ ____ with hari chutney is a common sight at all Delhi food festivals. Make the pa____ slightly bigger and you can enjoy them as morning breakfast too. 4-6 small ones can be made at one go on a single tawa for an interesting chaat party.

Serves 6   *Picture on page 94*

PANCAKE
1 cup dhuli moong dal (split, skinned moong beans) - wash & soak overnight
2 tbsp fresh curd (yogurt)
4 green chillies - cut into half lengthwise, deseeded and chopped
1 tbsp besan (gram flour)
a big pinch of hing (asafoetida)
½ tsp baking powder
1 tsp salt, ¼ tsp haldi, ¼ tsp garam masala

TOPPING
1½ onions - very finely chopped
200 gm paneer - crumbled or roughly mashed
2-3 tbsp very finely chopped coriander
1 tsp salt, 1 tsp chat masala, ¼ tsp red chilli powder

1. Wash dal. Soak dal overnight or for at least 4-5 hours in some water till soft.
2. Drain away the water and grind to a smooth paste with curd and green chillies.
3. Remove to a big mixing bowl. Add all other ingredients of the pancake.
4. Beat well with an electric mixer till very light and fluffy, for about 3-4 minutes.
5. Add about ¼ cup water to the paste to get a fairly thick batter, of a very thick pouring consistency, like that of a dosa.
6. Mix all ingredients of the topping and keep aside.
7. Heat 1 tbsp oil in a non-stick tawa or pan. Remove from fire. Pour 2 tbsp of batter (about half kadcchi) and spread quickly in a circular outer motion (like a dosa) to a small, thin pancake of 4-5" diameter. Do not keep it thick.
8. Sprinkle some topping mixture on the chillah and press gently.
9. Pour some oil on the sides. Pour some oil on the top also. Turn side and let it turn crisp from both sides. Remove from fire.
10. Fold into half, serve hot with hari chutney.

Kalmi Bare

Servings 15 pieces

SOAK TOGETHER FOR 3 HOURS IN WATER
1 cup channe ki dal (split gram)
¼ cup moong dhuli dal

CRUSH TOGETHER
1 tsp jeera (cumin seeds), 1 tsp saboot dhania (coriander seeds)
½ tsp crushed pepper corns (saboot kali mirch)

MIX TOGETHER
3 cups curds - beat well till smooth, 1 tsp powdered sugar
½ tsp red chilli powder, ¾ tsp salt, ¾ tsp bhuna jeera powder, ½ tsp kala namak

ACCOMPANIMENTS
imli ki saunth and hari chutney

OTHER INGREDIENTS
a pinch of hing
¼ cup chopped coriander
2 green chillies - chopped finely
½" ginger piece - chopped finely
1 onion - chopped finely
1 tsp salt
¼ tsp red chilli powder, garam masala & amchoor

1. Strain soaked dals.
2. Grind dals with just a few tbsp of water to a fine paste. Mix the dal with pinch of hing, chopped coriander, green chillies, ginger, onion, salt, red chilli powder, garam masala and amchoor. Mix well.
3. Crush together all the ingredients written under crush together and add to the dal mixture.
4. Add 1 tsp hot oil also to the paste. Beat well for 5 minutes.
5. Make 6 balls. Flatten them so that they are ½" thick.
6. Deep fry to a light pink colour. Cool for 15-20 minutes.
7. Cut each fried bare into 2 pieces. Refry in oil till golden.
8. Beat curd. Add all the ingredients to it. Keep aside.
9. To serve, dip each bare in curd and arrange in a flat dish.
10. Pour the remaining curd on the arranged bare. Sprinkle imli chutney and hari chutney over it in circles. Garnish with red chilli powder, bhuna jeera powder.

Dahi Bhalle

Delicious lentil dumplings in spiced yogurt, topped with roasted cashews and ground cumin.

Makes 25

1½ cups (250 gm) dhuli urad dal - washed
½" piece ginger - very finely chopped, 2-3 pinches of hing (asafoetida)
½ tsp salt, ½ tsp baking powder
1 tsp jeera (cumin seeds), oil for frying

MIX TOGETHER
3 cups curds - beat well till smooth, 1 tsp powdered sugar
½ tsp red chilli powder, ¾ tsp salt, 1 tsp bhuna jeera powder, ½ tsp kala namak

ACCOMPANIMENTS
imli ki saunth and hari chutney, page 91

1. Wash and soak dal in enough water to cover the dal, for about 3 hours.
2. Strain dal. Grind in a mixer in 2 batches, with chopped ginger and hing to a rough paste. Do not over grind. Add about ¼ cup water if required to grind. Keep scraping the dal on the sides, of the mixer while grinding.
3. Transfer dal paste to a deep pan or patila. Add salt and baking powder.
4. Beat well for 5-7 minutes with an electric hand mixer till the mixture turns whitish and frothy. Add ¼ -½ cup hot water while beating, enough to get a soft dropping consistency like that of a cake batter. Beat some more with the fingers to feel the mixture if it is light. To test if the mixture is ready, put a small drop of paste in a bowl of water. If it rises to the surface, it is done, otherwise beat some more.
5. Heat oil in a kadhai for deep frying. Wet the palm of your left hand. With wet hands, make bhalla with dal batter into 2" discs on the wet palm. Sprinkle some jeera seeds on it. Press lightly to stick the jeera and flatten the bhalla.
6. Deep fry 5-6 bhallas at a time in medium hot oil till they swell. Reduce heat to low and turn the side. Fry on low medium heat till light golden. Drain from oil, keep aside.
7. Beat curd. Add all the ingredients to the curd. Keep side.
8. Boil 6 cups water with 2 tsp salt. Remove from fire and add the bhallas. Soak in salted hot water for 5 minutes. Remove from water on to a plate.
9. After 5 minutes, press out water lightly. Dip in curd and arrange bhallas in a flat dish.
10. Pour the remaining curd on the arranged bhallas. Sprinkle imli chutney and hari chutney over it in circles. Garnish with red chilli powder, bhuna jeera powder and some roasted cashew bits (optional).

Matar Aur Kulche

The dry mattars (peas) look like channas (chick peas). Most popular with the masses and with the calorie conscious, coz it is made with very little oil. It's our favourite too!. Serve it with readymade kulchas which are very easily available in hygienic packs.

Picture on page 39   *Serves 4*

2 cups dry matar - soaked in water overnight, 2 tbsp oil
½ tsp jeera (cumin seeds), a pinch of hing (asafoetida), 1 tsp salt
1 tsp chaat masala powder, 1 tsp bhuna jeera powder (roasted cumin powder)
½ tsp garam masala powder, ½ tsp red chilli powder, ½ tsp amchoor

JAL JEERA WATER(YOU CAN BUY READY MADE PACKET ALSO)
½ of a small bunch poodina (25 gm)
a small lemon sized ball of seedless imli (tamarind) - washed well
1 tsp kala namak (black salt), ¾ tsp salt, 1 tsp jeera (cumin seeds)
5-6 tbsp saboot kali mirch (black peppercorns), ½ tsp saunf (fennel seeds)
½ tsp amchoor, a pinch of hing (asafoetida), 1 dry red chilli
seeds of 1 moti illaichi (black cardamom)

TOPPING
1 small onion - cut into ½, then slice into half rings widthwise to get thin strips
½ of a firm tomato - cut into thin strips, ½" piece of ginger - jullienes, (thin strips)
1 green chilli - cut into half lengthwise, deseeded and finely chopped
juice of ½ lemon, or to taste

1. Drain water from the soaked peas. Rub and wash again to discard any white skin. Put them in a pressure cooker. Add 1½ cups water. Pressure cook on high flame till two whistles and reduce flame and let it cook for 15 minutes. Remove from fire and let the pressure come down by itself.

2. Strain the matars to discard any water. Remove any of those thin white skins. Leave them in the strainer. Mash the channas with the back of a karchi.

3. To prepare the jal jeera water, grind all ingredients with 2 tbsp water to a paste. Remove to a bowl and add ½ cup water. Mix well and keep to rest for 3-4 hours. Strain through a muslin cloth (mal-mal ka kapda). You can buy a ready made packet of jal jeera and make about ½ cup of it. Keep aside.

4. To prepare the mattars, heat 2 tbsp oil in a kadhai. Add jeera. Remove from fire. Add hing, salt, and all the other masalas - chat masala, bhuna jeera, garam masala, red chilli powder and amchoor. Return to fire and stir for 30 seconds.

5. Add strained peas. Stir for 3-4 min. Add jal jeera and cook for another 2 minutes. Mix well. Remove from fire and keep aside till serving time.

6. To serve, heat mattar. Transfer to a dish. Sprinkle onion, tomato, ginger and green chilli. Squeeze lemon juice on it and mix lightly. Serve with kulchas.

Aloo Chaat

A common street food of Delhi. The crisp golden fried potatoes on the big iron griddle (tawa) is a common sight in Delhi. Do not fry the potatoes on high heat because they will never turn crisp. Also remember, sprinkle the masalas on the hot potatoes while they are still hot. The oil on the hot potatoes absorbs the masalas very well and the masala coats the potatoes nicely. It is better if the tawa is a little big as all the potatoes can be fried together. If the size is small, you can fry them in 2 batches. The first batch when done should not be removed from the tawa, but instead pushed to extreme ends of the tawa. Here the heat is not much, the potatoes remain hot and also turn crisp lying there. The next batch can be added in the centre of the tawa where there is oil.

Serves 3-4

4 potatoes of medium size - boiled
1 tbsp kala chaat masala or regular chaat masala
juice of 1 medium lemon
1 tsp bhuna jeera powder (roasted cumin powder)
¼ tsp red chilli powder
¼ tsp amchoor
½ tsp kala namak (rock salt)
½ tsp saboot kali mirch (pepper corns) - crushed

a few tooth picks - to serve, optional

1. Peel and cut boiled potatoes into 1" pieces.
2. Shallow fry the potato pieces in a frying pan or a non stick tawa in 5-6 tbsp oil on low medium heat till golden brown in colour. Keep turning sides with the help of a pair of tongs (chimta) to brown the potatoes evenly.
3. Remove the potatoes from oil in a bowl.
4. Sprinkle all the masalas immediately on the hot potatoes and toss well to mix all the ingredients. Serve with tooth picks in individual bowls.

Bhuna Jeera Powder (roasted cumin powder)

To make bhuna jeera powder, heat a tawa on fire. Put ½ cup jeera on it. Stir continuously on low heat till jeera starts to change colour and turns fragrant. Let it turn golden brown. Remove to a plate immediately. When it cools down, grind to a rough powder in a small mixer/ spice grinder. Store for a month in an air tight bottle.

Golgappe

Delicious golgappas stuffed with boiled chickpeas (channas) and potato, served with poodina pani. In other parts of the country, it is also known as "pani puri" or "poochkas".

Serves 4

DOUGH
½ cup fine suji, ½ cup maida (plain flour)

1. Mix suji and maida and knead a stiff dough with about ¼ cup water. Cover dough with wet muslin cloth (mal-mal ka kapda) and keep aside for 2 hours.
2. Take tiny marble sized balls of dough and roll each into thin puris of 1½" diameter.
3. Heat oil in a kadhai and fry puris immediately (puri should not get dry). Keep the dough covered. Fry puris on low heat, turning twice till golden brown. Store puris in an air tight container.

FILLING
½ cup boiled kabuli channe (safed chhole/chickpeas)
1 large potato - boiled & chopped
some imli (tamarind) chutney - see chutney section

POODINA PANI
50 gm pudina or mint leaves (1 big bunch), 2 tbsp fresh coriander leaves
1 green chilli, juice of one lemon
2 tsp black salt, 1½ tsp salt
1 tsp jeera (cumin seeds)
7-8 saboot kali mirch (black peppercorns)
½ tsp saunf (fennel seeds)

1. Grind all the ingredients of poodina pani to a fine paste.
2. Add 2 cups of water to this paste and mix well. Chill pani.
3. To serve, make a hole in the centre of a puri, fill some boiled channa and potato. Add a spoonful of tamarind chutney and fill it with poodina pani. Eat immediately.

Note: To make puris, you might get tempted to roll out a big round and then cut into smaller rounds with a sharp lid or a biscuit cutter. But this will not work. Although it is going to take longer, each puri has to be rolled individually.

Paapdi Chaat

Small flatten discs of flour, deep fried till crisp and golden. These are topped with whipped curd and mithi chutney. Usually a bhalla is also added to the paapdi chat.

Serves 4 (25 pieces)

DOUGH FOR PAAPDI
1 cup maida (plain flour)
1 cup wheat flour (whole wheat flour)
2 tsp ghee/oil
½ cup water
oil for frying

TOPPING
1 boiled potato - peeled and chopped
2 cups dahi - well beaten with ½ tsp salt and 1 tsp powdered sugar
some green chutney, tamarind chutney (see page 91)
1 tbsp fresh, red anar ke dane (fresh pomegranate kernels), optional
1 tsp bhuna jeera (roasted cumin) - powdered
1 tsp red chilli powder

1. To prepare the paapdi, mix maida and wheat flour. Add ghee/oil and rub with the finger tips. Add just enough water to make a stiff dough.
2. Roll small thin discs of 1½" diameter.
3. Prick them 2 to 3 times with a fork, so that they do not swell on frying.
4. Heat oil in a kadhai. Fry paapdi in 2- 3 batches, on low heat until light golden brown.
5. To serve, arrange the paapdi in a serving plate.
6. Spread boiled potatoes.
7. Sprinkle dahi well, so that each papdi is covered well with dahi.
8. Sprinkle some saunth and hari chutney.
9. Sprinkle some bhuna jeera and red chilli powder. Garnish with fresh anaar ke dane. Serve immediately.

Shakarkandi Seekh ki Chat

Serves 6-8

½ kg shakarkandi (sweet potatoes), (about 4 pieces)
8-10 kaju (cashewnuts) - chopped (2 tbsp)
2 tbsp khoya - crumbled (30 gm)
3 tbsp grated or mashed paneer (cottage cheese)
1 tsp finely chopped ginger
1 tbsp finely chopped poodina (mint leaves)
½ tsp garam masala powder, ½ tsp red chilli powder
¾ tsp black pepper powder (kali mirch), 1½ tsp salt
4 tbsp besan (gramflour)
TO SRRINKLE- 1 tsp chaat masala powder

1. Put shakarkandi in a pressure cooker. Pour enough water to cover. Pressure cook to give 2 whistles and then keep on low heat for 3-4 minutes. Remove from fire and let the pressure drop. Peel and mash the sweet potatoes. Keep aside.
2. Roast besan and kaju on a tawa for 2-3 minutes till fragrant.
3. Mix mashed sweet potatoes, khoya, paneer, ginger, poodina, garam masala powder, red chilli powder, kali mirch powder, salt and roasted besan and kaju.
4. Take a small ball of the mixture, Shape it like a 2" long seekh kebab.
5. Take a pencil or a skewer and push it carefully from one end of kebab to the other, without puncturing at any point.
6. Gently pull out skewer or the pencil. Keep the seekhs in the fridge for ½ hour.
7. To serve, deep fry the seekhs in medium hot oil in a kadhai to a light brown colour. Sprinkle chaat masala and serve hot with poodina-dahi chutney given below.

Dahi Poodina Chutney:

1. Hang 1½ cups curd for 15 minutes in a muslin cloth.
2. Grind ½ cup coriander, ½ cup mint, 2 green chillies, ½ onion and 2 flakes garlic with a little water to a paste. Beat the hung curd well till smooth. Add prepared green paste, 1 tsp oil, pinch of kala namak, ¼ tsp bhuna jeera and salt to taste. Mix, serve.

Dal ki Pakori : Recipe on page 44 ➤
Masala Kaju : Recipe on page 35 ➤

Fruit Chaat

Delicious, light and healthy! Although the name suggests only fruit, it also has vegetables like cucumber, tomato and yam (kachalu). Yam is a vegetable which looks like a potato but has a taste similar to colocasia (arbi). One of the best fruit chat is sold in the lane next to Shahjehan road. Serve it in pattals for the authentic look!

Serves 4

2 cups papaya (papita) - cut into 1" pieces
1 apple - cut into ½" pieces with the peel
½ cup green or black grapes
½ cup of cucumber (kheera) - cut into ½" pieces without the peel
½ tomato - cut into thin long pieces
½ banana (kela) - cut into round slices
½ kachaalu (yam) - boiled, optional
1 tbsp very finely chopped coriander, optional

OTHER INGREDIENTS
3½ tsp chat masala
1 tsp bhuna jeera powder (roasted cumin powder)
2 tbsp powdered sugar
juice of 1½ large lemons

1. To boil kachalu, put it in a pressure cooker. Cover with water. Pressure cook to give 1 whistle. Reduce heat and keep on low heat for 4-5 minutes. Remove from fire. Let it cool, Peel the kachalu and cut it into 4 pieces lengthwise. Cut each slice widthwise into thin slices, to get small triangular slices.
2. Put it in a big bowl. Mix all vegetables and fruit in the bowl.
3. Sprinkle chat masala, bhuna jeera, powdered sugar. Squeeze lemon juice over it. Toss lightly with a fork. Taste and adjust spices. Serve with toothpicks or small snack forks.

Note: Any fruits like watermelon, oranges, mangoes etc. can be added according to your choice and availability.

◄ Chhole Bhature : Recipe on page 30

Purani Dilli Ke
NASHTE AUR SNACKS

Aloo Seviyaan Roll

An extremely crisp snack coated with thin vermicelli (seviyaan).

Makes 16

2½ cups boiled and grated aloo (4 potatoes)
2 slices bread - churned in a mixer to get fresh bread crumbs
½ cup chopped coriander, ½ tsp chaat masala
½ tsp bhuna jeera (roasted cumin powder)
1½ tsp salt, ½ tsp pepper
½ tsp baking powder
2 tbsp melted butter

TO COAT
¼ cup maida, 1 cup very thin seviyaan- crushed roughly into small pieces by hand

1. Mix grated potatoes with coriander, chaat masala, fresh bread crumbs, bhuna jeera, salt and pepper. Mix gently without applying too much pressure.
2. Sprinkle baking powder on the potatoes. Melt butter in a microwave or on fire and pour on the potatoes. Mix gently but very well.
3. Make about 16 lemon sized balls. With a ball of the mixture, make a long oval roll. Shape to give a neat roll.
4. Flatten the ends of the roll by making it stand upright on a flat platform. To neaten the roll, roll the aloo roll on the flat platform.
5. Break seviyaan into very small pieces. Spread on a plate. Spread maida also on a separate plate.Take 1 cup of water separately in a shallow flat bowl (katori).
6. Press the roll over maida to coat all over.
7. Dip the roll in the water for a second and then immediately roll it over the seviyaan. All the sides should be completely covered with seviyaan. Stick the seviyaan well.
8. Keep aside to set for atleast 15 minutes. Deep fry 2-3 pieces at a time. Serve with poodina chutney.

Bervi Poori aur Aloo Chhole

From the famous Kedarnath Premchand Halwai of Chandani Chowk.
Serve the aloos with kachouri, samosa or crisp fried poories. An ultimate breakfast.

Picture on cover   *Makes 16-18*

SUBZI

1½ cups kabuli channa (safeed choole) - soaked overnight for 6-8 hours
1 potato
¼ tsp cooking soda (soda-bi- carb)
4 tbsp oil/ghee
2 pinches of hing (asafoetida)
½ tsp jeera (cumin seeds), ½ tsp fenugreek seeds (methi daana)
1 green chilli - finely chopped
1 tsp ginger paste (1" piece of ginger - crushed to a paste)
½ tsp haldi, 1 tbsp dhania powder
1 tsp channa masala (readymade)
1½ tsp salt, ½ tsp amchoor, ½ tsp red chilli powder
1 tsp lemon juice, 2 tbsp coriander leaves - chopped

POORI (DOUGH)

2 cups atta (whole wheat flour)
½ cup sooji (semolina) - soaked in 1 cup water
2 tbsp ghee

FILLING OF POORI

¾ cup dhuli urad ki dal (white dal)
a pinch hing (asafoetida)
½ tsp saunf (fennel seeds)
2 tsp finely chopped ginger
3 tsp dhania powder, ¾ tsp red chilli powder, ½ tsp salt
oil for frying

1. Soak the channa over night in some water. Drain water. Add 3 cups fresh water. Add soda. Mix well. Pressure cook till one whistle on high flame and then keep on low heat for 15 minutes. Remove from fire.
2. Boil and peel potato, then cut into 6 pieces. Keep aside.
3. For filling of puris, soak dal in 2 cups water for atleast 2-3 hours.
4. For the dough, soak sooji in 1 cup water for 1 hour.

5. For the subzi, heat 4 tsbp oil/ghee in a kadhai, reduce heat, add hing, jeera and methi daana. Do not let the methi seeds turn black. Add green chillies.

6. Then add the ginger paste and stir for 30 seconds. Add haldi, dhania powder and channa masala. Bhuno for 2 minutes.

7. Add potatoes and stir for 2-3 minutes. Add channas, salt, amchoor and red chilli powder. Cook for 15 minutes on medium heat.

8. Add coriander and lemon juice. Remove from fire. Keep aside till serving time.

9. For the poories, mix atta with the soaked sooji. Add ghee and mix well. Knead into a dough as for poories. Keep the dough aside, covered with a moist napkin or cloth.

10. For the filling of poories, drain the soaked dal. Grind it to a paste in a mixer-grinder to a paste, using very little water if required.

11. Heat 2 tbsp ghee in a kadhai. Add hing and saunf. Wait till saunf starts to change colour. Add finely chopped ginger, dhania powder, red chilli powder and salt. Bhuno for 1 minute. Add the dal paste. Bhuno for 5 minutes. Let it cool.

12. Make small lemon sized balls of the dough. Roll out a little. Put 1 heaped teaspoon of dal filling. Make a ball again. Roll out to a puri.

13. Deep fry in hot oil. Serve with aloo-chole ki sabzi.

Mattar Kachouri aur Subzi

Enjoy this subzi with kachouris, poories or paranthas! It's good fun to have it with buttered toasts for breakfast too.

Picture on page 94   *Makes 12-14*

DOUGH FOR KACHOURI
2 cups maida (flour)
½ tsp baking powder, ½ tsp salt
2 tbsp ghee
½ cup warm water to knead, approx.

FILLING
2 cups peas (matar) - shelled
1 tbsp ghee
2 pinches of hing (asafoetida)
¼ tsp jeera (cumin seeds), 1 tsp dhania powder, ¼ tsp haldi (turmeric powder)
¼ tsp grated ginger
1 green chilli - deseeded and chopped
1 tsp salt, ¼ tsp red chilli powder, ¾ tsp chaat masala
¾ tsp amchoor, ¾ tsp garam masala
2 tbsp besan (gramflour)

SUBZI
6 potatoes - boiled, peeled and cut into 5-6 pieces, mash the pieces roughly
3½ tbsp ghee or oil
3 pinches of hing (asafoetida)
¾ tsp jeera (cumin seeds), 1 tsp saunf (fennel)
¼ tsp methi dana (fenugreek seeds)
½ tsp haldi powder, 1 tsp dhania powder
1½ tsp salt, ¾ tsp red chilli powder
1 tbsp aam ke achar ka masala
1 green chilli - finely chopped
2 tbsp chopped coriander (hara dhania)
1 tsp very finely chopped or grated ginger

1. To prepare the dough, sift maida, baking powder and salt through a sieve (channi).
2. Add ghee and mix well till it appears like bread crumbs. Knead well with warm water into a soft dough. Keep aside for 20 minutes.
3. For the filling, boil 4-5 cups water with 1 tsp salt and 1 tsp sugar. Add peas to boiling water. As soon as the boil returns, remove from fire. Let peas be in hot

water for 15 minutes. Strain and keep aside. Mash lightly with the back of a big spoon or a potato masher.

4. Heat ghee in a kadhai, add hing and jeera. Reduce heat. When jeera turns golden, add dhania powder, haldi and grated ginger. Bhuno for 1 minute.

5. Add the chopped green chillies, mix and cook for 2 minutes.

6. Add peas to the above masala in the kadhai, mix well and bhuno till golden, for about 10 minutes on low heat.

7. Add the salt, red chilli powder, chaat masala, amchoor, garam masala and besan. Bhuno for another 2 minutes. Remove from fire. Cool the filling.

8. With the dough, make small puries and fill each with 1 tbsp mattar masala. Cover to form a ball and flatten it slightly.

9. Heat oil in a kadhai and deep fry 5-6 pieces at a time. The oil should be hot when you first drop the kachouries in oil, then lower flame and cook till they turn brown.

10. For the subzi, heat ghee in a kadhai. Reduce heat and add hing, jeera, saunf and methi dana.

11. When methi dana turns brown, add haldi, dhania powder, salt and red chilli powder. Bhuno for 1 minute on low heat.

12. Add achar ka masala. Stir for another 1 minute.

13. Add the potatoes, chopped green chilli, coriander and ginger. Stir fry on medium heat for 3-4 minutes.

14. Add 3 cups of water. Bring to a boil. Reduce heat and cook for another 10 minutes. Remove from fire. Serve hot.

Variation : Aloo Hing Kachouri

Use 2 medium sized potatoes - boiled and grated instead of matar, for the filling. Rest all the ingredients remain the same. Proceed in the same way as for matar kachouri.

Chhole Bhature

Awesome! I can never forget the channa bhaturas I used to have at "Sadar Bazar" when I went for cracker shopping for my kids for Diwali.

Picture on page 22   Serves 4

PRESSURE COOK TOGETHER
1 cup channa kabuli (Bengal gram)
¼ tsp soda- bi-carb (mitha soda)
2 moti illaichi (big cardamoms), 1" stick dalchini (cinnamon)
2 tsp tea leaves tied in a muslin cloth or 2 tea bags, 1 tsp salt

MASALA
2 onions - chopped finely
1½ tsp anar daana (dry pomegranate seeds) - powdered
5 big tomatoes - chopped finely
1" piece ginger - chopped finely, 1 green chilli - chopped finely
1 tsp dhania powder, ½ tsp garam masala
½ tsp red chilli powder or to taste
2 tsp channa masala, 1¼ tsp salt or to taste

BHATURE
2 cups maida (plain flour), 1 cup suji (semolina)
½ tsp salt, ½ tsp sugar, ½ tsp soda-bi-carb (mitha soda)
½ cup curd, (preferably a day old and slightly sour)
oil for deep frying

1. Soak channas overnight or for 6-8 hours in a pressure cooker. Next morning, discard water. Wash channas with fresh water and add mitha soda, moti illaichi, dalchini, tea leaves, 1 tsp salt and just enough water to cover the channas nicely.
2. Pressure cook all the ingredients together to give one whistle. After the first whistle, keep on low flame for about 15 minutes. Remove from fire. Keep aside.
3. Heat 4 tbsp oil. Add onions. Saute till transparent. Add anardaana powder. Cook stirring till onions turn brown. (Do not burn them).
4. Add chopped tomatoes, ginger and green chill. Stir fry for 5- 6 minutes.
5. Add dhania powder, garam masala and chilli powder. Mash and stir fry tomatoes occasionally for 8- 10 minutes or till they turn brown in colour and oil separates.
6. Strain channas, reserving the liquid. Remove tea bag from the boiled channas.
7. Add the strained channas to the onion-tomato masala. Mix well. Stir fry gently for 5-7 minutes.
8. Add channa masala. Add the channa liquid. Check salt and add a little to taste. Cook for 15-20 minutes on medium heat till the liquid dries up and still a saucy consistency remains. Keep aside.

9. For bhature, soak suji in ¾ cup warm water, which is just enough to cover it. Keep aside for 10 minutes.
10. Sift salt, sugar, soda and maida in a paraat or a shallow bowl.
11. Add sugar, soaked suji and curd. Mix very well. Add warm water little by little, mixing well till the dough collects in the centre. Knead well to make a firm dough. Do not make it loose as on keeping it turns loose.
12. Knead again with greased hands till the dough is smooth. Pat some oil on the dough to prevent it from drying. Grease a polythene with oil from inside and put the dough in it. Tie a knot loosely. Keep it in a warm place for 3-4 hours or till serving time.
13. Make 8-10 balls. Roll each ball to an oblong shape. Pull from one side to get a pointed tip. Deep fry in hot oil. Drain on paper napkins. Serve with channas.

Paneer Pakore (Special)

Serves 4

250 gm paneer, some chaat masala to sprinkle

FILLING
1 small onion - grated and squeezed well
1" ginger piece - grated and crushed to a paste (1 tsp)
3-4 flakes garlic - crushed to a paste (½ tsp)
½ tsp chilli powder, ½ tsp garam masala, ½ tsp ajwain (carom seeds)
½ tsp salt, 1 tsp dhania powder, 1 tsp amchoor

BATTER
1 cup besan, 1/3 cup water - approx., 2 tbsp chopped coriander
2 pinches baking powder, ¾ tsp each red chilli powder and salt, or to taste

1. Cut paneer into 1½" squares which are slightly thicker than ¼" thickness.
2. Slit the pieces of paneer, a little more than halfway but not till the end.
3. Sprinkle some chaat masala on them on both sides.
4. To prepare the filling, mix all ingredients of the filling together.
5. With the help of the knife insert some filling in slit of the paneer pieces. Press well.
6. Make a thick batter with all the ingredients. Beat well and keep aside for 10 minutes.

Paneer Pakore

7. Dip the stuffed pieces of paneer in the batter and deep fry in hot oil till golden.
8. Serve hot sprinkled with chaat masala.

Gobhi Samosa

Picture on page 58   *Serves 8-10*

DOUGH
¾ cup plain flour (maida), ¼ cup fine semolina (suji)
¼ tsp salt, a pinch of baking powder
2 tbsp ghee or butter or margarine

VEGETABLE FILLING
1 medium cauliflower - grated (2 cups)
1 boiled potato - mashed coarsely (½ cup)
½" piece fresh ginger - grated
salt to taste, ½ tsp red chilli powder
1 tsp roasted, ground cumin seeds (bhuna jeera)
¼ tsp amchoor
1 tbsp each of cashews (kaju) and raisins (kishmish) - chopped
2 green chillies - deseeded and finely chopped, ¼ tsp sugar

1. Sift flour, semolina, salt and baking powder into a bowl. Rub in ghee or butter. Add a few tablespoons of cold water to form a firm dough. Knead for 5-7 minutes until the dough becomes smooth and elastic. Cover the dough and keep aside for 30 minutes or longer while making the filling.

2. To prepare filling, heat 3 tbsp oil in a pan. Remove from heat. Add ginger, salt, red chilli powder, bhuna jeera and amchoor.

3. Return to heat. Add kaju and kishmish. Cook for a few seconds. Add potatoes. Stir for a few seconds. Add cauliflower. Mix well. Add sugar and green chillies.

4. Cover and cook on low heat till the cauliflower is cooked. Make the filling spicy if you like. Keep aside.

5. Make lemon sized balls of dough. Roll out into thin rounds. Cut each circle in half. Brush some water on straight edges. Pick up the half circle & form a cone shape, overlapping straight edges ¼ inch & pressing firmly to seal the seam. Fill cone two-thirds with filling, about 1 tbsp of the filling in each cone.

6. Press together to make a secure joint.

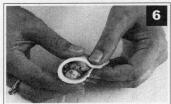

7. Deep fry 8-10 pieces on low medium heat till golden. Drain on paper and serve with chutney.

TIP: Never fry the samosas on high heat and fry 8-10 pieces together in a single batch. If the oil is too hot, the outer covering gets browned very fast, without getting cooked properly.

Paneer Roll

Makes 8 Rolls

250 gm paneer - grated (2 cups)
1 green chilli - deseeded and very finely chopped
1 tbsp very finely chopped coriander
1 tsp black pepper powder, ¾ tsp salt, 1 tsp chat masala, ½ tsp bhuna jeera
2 slices of bread - churned in a mixer to get fresh bread crumbs
4-5 tbsp grated cheese, ½ tsp baking powder, oil for frying

TO COAT
4 tbsp maida, ½ cup dry bread crumbs - very finely ground in a mixer and sifted through a soup strainer

1. Tear bread into pieces and churn in a mixer to get fresh crumbs.

2. Mix grated paneer, green chilli, coriander, cheese, pepper, salt, chat masala, bhuna jeera and bread crumbs. Sprinkle baking powder on the mixture. Mix well, mashing with the palms till very smooth.

3. Divide the mixture into 8 equal portions. Shape each portion into a ball.

4. Shape each ball into a roll, about 2" long. Flatten the sides of the roll, by pressing the sides of the roll against a flat surface. Lay the roll over a smooth kitchen platform and roll forwards and backwards to give it a smooth, neat look. Keep aside.

5. Spread maida & bread crumbs in separate flat plates. Take 1 cup of water separately in a shallow bowl (katori). Press roll over maida to coat. Then dip the roll in the water for a second and then immediately roll it over the dry bread crumbs. All the sides should be completely covered with bread crumbs.

6. Heat oil in a kadhai and fry 2 rolls a time till golden brown. Serve with hari chutney.

Note: To make dry bread crumbs instantly, break 2 slices of bread into pieces and place on a micro proof plate. Microwave for 2 minutes. Mix with the fingers to change sides and again microwave for 1 minute. Keep the slightly wet bread for 5 minutes to dry out and turn crisp. Grind in a mixer grinder to get fresh instant, dry bread crumbs.

Kathi Roti

These rolls are served with paneer-vegetable sticks. For a quicker version omit the paneer sticks and serve just the subzi with roomali roti, although the sticks definitely add to its taste. The sticks can be served separately as a snack too.

Picture on page 1   *Serves 4*

SUBZI
1 cup nutri nugget granules - soaked for 1 hour and drained
½ cup matar (peas) - boiled
1 cup tomato puree, 1 tomato - chopped
1 onion - chopped
2 pinches of hing, ½ tsp jeera (cumin seeds)
1 dry saboot red chilli - crushed
½ tsp garm masala, 1 tbsp dhania powder, 1 tsp salt
½ tsp amchoor, ¼ tsp red chilli powder
1 green chilli - finely chopped
juice of ½ lemon
1 tsp ginger-garlic paste
2 tbsp pao bhaji masala
2 tbsp coriander leaves - chopped

PANEER-VEG STICKS
125 gms paneer- cut into ½" thick slices and then into ¾" squares
1 capsicum- cut into 1" pieces
1 tomato - cut into 4 pieces lengthwise, pulp removed and cut into 1" pieces
some chaat masala

BATTER
1 cup besan (gramflour)
1/3 cup water - approx
2 pinches baking powder, ¾ tsp each red chilli powder and salt, or to taste
1 green chilli - chopped very finely

1. For the subzi, soak the nuti nuggets in 1 cup water, keep aside for ½ hour. Strain through a soup strainer. Wash several times with water in the strainer itself. Press the nuggets in the strainer, squeezing out excess water from the nuggets.
2. Heat 4 tbsp ghee or oil in a kadhai, add hing, jeera, green chillies and saboot sookhi lal mirch. Wait for 30 seconds.
3. Add chopped onion and cook till golden.
4. Add the nutri nuggets granules and bhuno for 5 minutes.
5. Add the peas, ginger paste, dhania powder, salt, pao bhaji masala and chopped tomatoes. Bhuno for 5 minutes.

6. Add tomato puree, red chilli powder and amchoor. Mix well and cook for 5 minutes.

7. Add 1 cup water mix thoroughly. Give one boil. Simmer for 5 minutes till a semi dry masala is ready. Add coriander and mix. Remove from fire. Keep aside.

8. For the sticks, make a thick batter with all the ingredients. Beat well and keep aside for 10 minutes.

9. Sprinkle chat masala nicely on paneer, capsicum & tomato pieces. Mix lightly.

10. Thread a capsicum (wrong side facing you), then a paneer and then a tomato piece (right side facing you) on each tooth pick. Keep aside till serving time.

11. Heat oil for deep frying. Dip the paneer sticks in the prepared batter. Coat well with the fingers, sticking the batter nicely. Deep fry till golden.

12. To serve, sprinkle sticks with some chaat masala. Add lemon juice to the subzi. Serve subzi topped with a hot stick with roomali roti.

Masala Kaju

It is important to fry the cashews carefully as they turn brown very fast Keep stirring all the time while frying, till they change colour, for about a minute. Shut off the flame and start removing them from oil. Do not wait till all of them turn golden.

Serves 4-5   *Picture on page 21*

1 cup (100 gm) cashewnuts (kaju)
¾ tsp black pepper powder, preferably freshly ground
¼ tsp amchoor, 1½ tsp chat masala, ¼ tsp garam masala, ¼ tsp red chilli powder

1. Mix all the masalas together and keep ready. Heat 2 cups oil for frying. Reduce heat. Add kajus and stir fry continuously till they start changing colour and turn light golden. Shut off the flame. Remove from oil in a big bowl.

2. Immediately sprinkle the masalas while the kajus are still hot. Mix thoroughly with the fingers. Mix again after 2-3 minutes. Let it cool down.

3. When cool, store in air tight container. Serve with drinks.

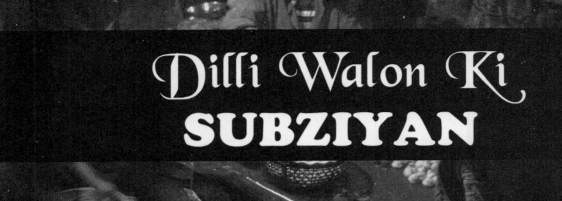

Dilli Walon Ki
SUBZIYAN

Karari Arvi

Serves 6

Crisp fried colocassia (arbi) with a fragrant flavour of carom seeds (ajwain). An excellent side dish.

½ kg arvi (colocassia)
oil for frying
1½ tsp ajwain (carom seeds)
2-3 pinches of hing (asafoetida)
1½ tsp salt, ¾ tsp red chilli powder

1. Put the arvi in a presure cooker. Add enough water to cover the arbi. Pressure cook to give 1 whistle. Reduce heat and cook for 2 minutes on low heat. Remove from fire and let the pressure drop by itself.
2. Peel the arvi and cut each into 2 pieces lengthwise. Flatten each piece.
3. Heat oil for frying in a kadhai. Deep fry arvi in 3-4 batches till golden brown. Remove from oil.
4. Heat 3 tbsp oil. Add ajwain and shut off the flame. Ad hing, salt and red chilli powder. Return to fire. Stir.
5. Add fried arvi. Mix very well. Reduce heat. Cover and cook on low heat for 5 minutes, stirring once or twice in between. Serve.

Shahi Paneer

Serves 4

**250 gm paneer - cut into 1" cubes, 5 large (500 gm) tomatoes
2 tbsp desi ghee or butter and 2 tbsp oil
4-5 flakes garlic and 1" piece ginger - ground to a paste (1½ tsp ginger-garlic paste)
1 tbsp kasoori methi (dry fenugreek leaves), 1 tsp tomato ketchup
½ tsp jeera (cumin seeds), 2 tsp dhania powder, ½ tsp garam masala
1 tsp salt, or to taste, ½ tsp red chilli powder, preferably degi mirch
½ cup water, ½-1 cup milk, approx., ½ cup cream (optional)
3 tbsp cashewnuts (kaju)**

1. Soak kaju in a little warm water for 10-15 minutes.
2. Drain kaju. Grind in a mixer to a very smooth paste using about 2 tbsp water.
3. Cut each tomato into 4 pieces. Boil tomatoes in ½ cup water. Simmer for 4-5 minutes on low heat till tomatoes turn soft. Remove from fire and cool. Cut each into 4 pieces. Grind the tomatoes along with the water to a smooth puree.
4. Heat oil and ghee or butter in a kadhai. Reduce heat. Add jeera. When it turns golden, add ginger-garlic paste.
5. When paste starts to change colour add the above tomato puree & cook till dry.
6. Add kasoori methi and tomato ketchup.
7. Add masalas - dhania powder, garam masala, salt and red chilli powder. Mix well for a few seconds. Cook till oil separates.
8. Add cashew paste. Mix well for 2 minutes.
9. Add water. Boil. Simmer on low heat for 4-5 minutes. Reduce heat.
10. Add the paneer cubes. Remove from fire. Keep aside to cool for about 5 minutes.
11. Add enough milk to the cold paneer masala to get a thick curry, mix gently. (Remember to add milk only after the masala is no longer hot, to prevent the milk from curdling. After adding milk, heat curry on low heat.)
12. Heat on low heat. Stir continuously till just about to boil.
13. Add cream, keeping the heat very low and stirring continuously. Remove from fire immediately and transfer to a serving dish. Swirl 1 tbsp cream over the hot paneer in the dish. Serve immediately.

Anghiti Tamatar

Picture on facing page   *Serves 4*

4-5 medium sized tomatoes - washed
½ onion - finely chopped, 1 tbsp butter
¼ cup peas (matar), ½ cup finely chopped carrot
¾ tsp dhania powder, ½ tsp garam masala
¼ red chilli powder, ¼ tsp haldi powder, ½ tsp salt
½ cup grated paneer

GRAVY
2 onions - sliced, 1 tomato - chopped
1" piece ginger - chopped (1 tbsp)
1 tsp salt, 1 tsp dhania powder, ½ tsp garam masala
¼ tsp amchoor, ¼ tsp red chilli powder, or to taste

1. From the stem side of the tomato, cut a piece like a lid and scoop out the pulp. Keep the lid aside. Rub the inside with a little salt, turn tomato upside down and leave for 10 minutes.

2. Heat 1 tbsp butter in a kadhai. Add chopped onion and bhuno till golden. Add the peas and carrots, dhania powder, garam masala, red chilli powder, haldi powder and salt. Cover and cook on medium flame for 5-7 minutes or till peas are cooked. Add the grated paneer. Remove from heat.

3. Fill this mixture in the tomatoes. Put the lid back. Secure with a toothpick. Hold each tomato on the flame with the help of tongs and roast for 3- 4 minutes till black patches appear. Repeat with the remaining tomatoes.

4. For the gravy, heat 4 tbsp oil and add sliced onions. Stir till golden brown. Add chopped tomatoes and ginger and cook for 7 minutes till tomatoes turn soft.

5. Add all masalas and cook for 2 minutes. Remove from fire and cool. Blend to a paste in a mixer grinder with ½ cup water.

6. Put prepared onion - tomato paste back in the same kadhai and stir for 4-5 minutes on low heat. Add enough warm water (1 cup) to get a thin gravy. Boil. Simmer for 5-7 minutes till you get a thick gravy and oil separates. Keep aside.

7. To serve, boil gravy and add the tomatoes. Give 1-2 quick boils. Serve hot.

Matar aur Kulcha : Recipe on page 16 ➤

Gobhi Fry

Fried cauliflower florets put in a delicious masala

Serves 4 　　　　　*Picture on opposite page*

1 medium whole cauliflowers (500 gms) - cut into medium size florets with stalks

MASALA
4 tbsp oil
3 onions - chopped
3 tomatoes - roughly chopped, 1" ginger - chopped
seeds of 1 moti illaichi, 3-4 saboot kali mirch (peppercorns) and 2 laung (cloves)
2 tbsp curd - beat well till smooth
½ tsp red chilli powder, ½ tsp garam masala, ½ tsp haldi, ½ tsp amchoor
1 tsp salt, or to taste

1. Break the cauliflower into medium size florets, keeping the stalk intact. Wash and pat dry on a kitchen towel.

2. Heat oil in a kadhai for deep frying. Add all the cauliflower pieces and fry to a light brown colour. Remove from oil and keep aside.

3. Heat 4 tbsp oil in a clean kadhai. Add chopped onion. Cook till onions turn golden brown.

4. Add moti illaichi, saboot kali mirch and laung. After a minute add chopped tomatoes and ginger. Cook for 4-5 minutes till they turn soft and masala turns little dry.

5. Add well beaten curd. Cook till masala turns reddish again.

6. Reduce heat. Add red chilli powder, garam masala, haldi, amchoor and salt. Cook for 1 minute. Add ½ cup water to get a thick masala. Boil. Cook for 1 minute on low flame. Keep aside.

7. At the time of serving, heat the masala. Add the fried cauliflower pieces to the masala and mix well on low heat for 2 minutes till the vegetable gets well blended with the masala. Serve hot.

Kale Angoor ki Baraf : Recipe on page 85

Dum Aloo

Golden fried aloos in a delicious Mughlai gravy.

Serves 4-6

POTATOES

20 small baby potatoes or 4 medium round potatoes - cut into 1" pieces
oil for frying

GRAVY

1 tej patta, 1 tsp shah jeera (black cumin)
4 tbsp very finely grated khoya
1½ tbsp kasoori methi (dry fenugreek leaves)
1½ tsp salt or to taste, ½ tsp garam masala

ONION PASTE (GRIND TOGETHER)

1 onion, 2 laung, ¾" piece of ginger, 4-5 flakes of garlic
seeds of 2 chhoti illaichi, 2 tsp saunf, seeds of 2 moti illaichi, 1" stick dalchini

TOMATO PASTE (GRIND TOGETHER)

4 tomatoes - blanched (boiled in hot water for 3-4 minutes and peeled)
¼ tsp jaiphal, ¼ tsp javitri, 2 dry, red chillies
2 tbsp kaju (cashewnuts)

1. Peel and wash the potatoes. Prick with a fork. Cut into 1" pieces, if using regular potatoes.
2. Keep the potatoes in salted water for 15 minutes. Strain and pat dry on a clean kitchen towel.
3. Heat oil and deep fry all potatoes together till they get cooked properly and are golden brown in colour. Take out 1 piece from oil and check to see if cooked. If done, then remove all pieces from the kadhai on paper napkins. Keep aside till serving time.
4. Grind all the ingredients of onion paste to a smooth paste. Keep aside.
5. Boil tomatoes in water for 3-4 minutes. Peel. Grind all the ingredients of tomato paste to a smooth paste. Keep aside.
6. For gravy - heat 3 tbsp oil, add tej patta and shah jeera, wait for a minute.
7. Add onion paste. Cook for 2-3 minutes till golden brown.
8. Add tomato paste. Stir for 8-10 minutes or till dry.

9. Add khoya, kasoori methi, salt and garam masala. Cook for 2 minutes, stirring. Add ¾ cup of water. Boil. Simmer for 3 minutes. Remove from fire and keep aside till serving time.
10. At serving time, add 1 cup milk and boil on low heat.
11. Add fried potatoes. Keep on fire for 2-3 minutes. Serve hot.

Dal Fry

The yellow tadka dal.

Serves 4

M   B

¼ cup arhar dal, ¾ cup channa dal
½ tsp haldi, 1½ tsp salt, 1 tsp kasoori methi, 1 tsp ghee

TADKA
3-4 tbsp ghee, ½ tsp tsp jeera, a pinch of hing
½ tsp chopped garlic, 1 onion - finely chopped
1 tsp finely chopped ginger, 2 tomatoes - finely chopped
½ tsp garam masala, 1 tsp dhania powder, 1/8 tsp amchoor
½ tsp red chilli powder, preferably degi mirch
1 tsp kasoori methi (dry fenugreek leaves), 1-2 whole green chillies

1. Clean and wash dals together in 2-3 changes of water. Add 3½ cups water, salt, haldi and 1 tsp kasoori methi. Pressure cook to give 1 whistle. Keep on low heat for 5 minutes. Remove from fire. Let the pressure drop by itself.
2. To prepare the tadka, heat ghee in a clean kadhai. Reduce heat. Add jeera. When it starts changing colour, add hing. Add garlic and stir for 30 seconds, till it just starts to change colour.
3. Add onions and stir till golden brown. Add ginger and chopped tomatoes. Stir for 2 minutes.
4. Add masalas and kasoori methi. Stir till tomatoes blend well with the masala, for about 3-4 minutes on low heat. Add green chillies. Mix well.
5. Pour over the hot dal and mix. Serve hot.

Dal ki Pakori

Lentil dumplings in a thin curry.

Picture on page 21   *Serves 5-6*

½ cup (200 gm) dhuli mung ki dal (husked green beans)
½ cup channe ki dal
½ tsp salt, ½ tsp eno fruit salt
oil for deep frying
GRAVY
3 tbsp ghee or 4 tbsp oil
2 onions - chop 1 onion and ground the second one to a paste in a mixer
2 tsp ginger-garlic paste
1 tsp salt, ½ tsp garam masala, 1½ tsp dhania powder, ½ tsp haldi powder
½ tsp red chilli powder, ¼ tsp amchoor
2 tomatoes - blanched (put in boiling water for 2-3 minutes and peeled) and pureed
2 tbsp chopped coriander

1. Wash dals and soak in water overnight.
2. Next day drain dals and grind them to a rough paste in a mixer grinder. Do not make it into a smooth paste. Beat ground dal in a bowl with an electric hand mixer for 5-7 minutes till it feels really light and frothy. To check it it is done put a small ball in a bowl of water. If it rises to the surface, it is done, otherwise beat some more. Add eno fruit salt and salt. Mix well.

3. Heat oil in a kadhai for deep frying. To test if oil is hot enough, drop a little paste into the kadhai. It should rise to the surface almost immediately.
4. Using wet fingers drop small amounts of paste into oil. Reduce heat to medium. When bubbles appear on the surface and they swell a little, turn and fry till golden yellow. Drain and keep aside.

5. For the gravy, heat oil or ghee. Add chopped onion and stir fry till golden.
6. Add ground onion paste and ginger-garlic paste. Stir for 3-4 minutes on low heat.
7. Add masalas - salt, garam masala, dhania powder, haldi, red chilli powder and amchoor. Stir on low heat for 1-2 minutes.
8. Add tomato puree. Stir on low heat for 7-8 minutes till the masala is well blended.
9. Add 4 cups water. Bring to a boil. Simmer the curry on low heat for 5-7 minutes.
10. At serving time, add the fried pakories and fresh coriander. Boil. Cover and cook for 4-5 minutes on low heat. The gravy should be quite thin. Serve.

Sabut Simla Mirch

Serves 4   *Picture on page 2*

4 small capsicums
1 onion - finely chopped
3 potatoes - boiled and mashed roughly
2 tsp grated ginger
1 green chilli - finely chopped, 2 tbsp chopped coriander
3 tbsp oil
1 tsp jeera (cumin seeds)
½ tsp haldi, 1 tsp dhania powder, ¼ tsp amchoor, ½ tsp garam masala
½ tsp red chilli powder, ¾ tsp salt, or taste
a few tooth picks

1. Wash and cut a slice from the top of each capsicum like a small lid. Keep the lids with their respective capsicums. (Do not mix all the lids).
2. Heat 3 tbsp oil in a kadhai. Add jeera. When it turns golden, add onions. Stir fry till golden. Add ginger, stir fry for 1 minute.
3. Add haldi, dhania, amchoor, garam masala, red chilli powder and salt.
4. Add mashed potatoes, green chilli and coriander. Mix well and bhuno for another 4-5 minutes. Remove from fire and cool.
5. Stuff this mixture in the capsicum. Place lids back. Secure lids with tooth picks.
6. In a kadhai/pan put 2 tbsp oil and shallow fry the capsicums on low heat for about 15 minutes. Keep them spread out, turning sides occassionally, till the skin becomes brownish at some places and changes colour and becomes soft. Serve hot.

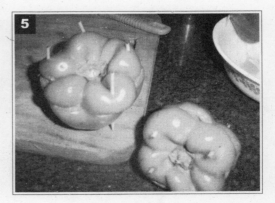

Vegetable Korma

Picture on page 4

Serves 4

2 slices of tinned pineapple - cut into 1" pieces
1 flower of cauliflower(200 gms)- cut into 1" flat pieces and fried till golden
4-5 french beans - cut into ½" diagonal pieces
½ cup shelled peas (matar)
2 small carrots - cut into round slices
4 tbsp oil, 2 onions - chopped finely
¼ tsp haldi (turmeric) powder, ½ tsp garam masala, 2 tsp salt

GRIND TOGETHER (CASHEW-CURD PASTE)
4 tsp khus-khus (poppy seeds) - soaked in warm water for 30 minutes and drained
¾ cup curd (dahi)
2 tbsp cashewnuts (kaju)
2 tbsp grated coconut (fresh or desiccated)
2 whole dry red chillies (sabut sookhi lal mirch)
½" piece ginger, 3-4 flakes garlic
2 tsp saboot dhania saboot, seeds of 2-3 chhoti illaichi (green cardamom)

1. Soak khus-khus, kaju, coconut, red chillies, ginger, garlic, saboot dhania and chhoti illaichi with little water. Keep aside for 15 minutes.
2. Drain and grind together to a paste along with curd. Keep aside the paste.
3. Cut cauliflower into 1" flat pieces and deep fry till golden.
4. Heat 4 tbsp oil. Add chopped onions. Cook till onions turn golden. Add haldi. Stir to mix well.
5. Add the prepared cashew- curd paste. Cook on low heat for 3-4 minutes.
6. Add beans, peas and carrots. Stir for 2 minutes.
7. Add 1 cup water or enough to get a thick gravy. Boil.
8. Add garam masala and salt. Simmer for 5 minutes.
9. Add fried cauliflower and pineapple pieces. Boil for 1 minute. Serve hot.

Dilli Style Sukhe Aloo

Serves

4 large potatoes - boiled, peeled and each cut into 8-12 pieces (1" cubes)
¾ tsp garam masala
½ tsp amchoor powder
2 tsp dhania powder
½ tsp haldi powder
½ tsp bhuna jeera powder (roasted cumin powder)
1¼ tsp salt or to taste

OTHER INGREDIENTS
4 tbsp oil
1 tsp jeera (cumin seeds)
1 tsp finely chopped ginger, 1 tsp finely chopped garlic
2 onions - thinly sliced
2 green chillies - cut into thin long pieces
3-4 tbsp coriander leaves - finely chopped
1 tsp lemon juice

1. Cut potatoes into medium sized cubes.
2. Heat 4 tbsp oil in kadhai, reduce heat and add jeera. When it starts to change colour, add ginger and garlic. Stir for ½ minute.
3. Add sliced onion and fry till onions turn golden brown.
4. Add green chilli pieces, stir for 1 minute.
5. Add the potatoes, garam masala, amchoor powder, dhania powder, haldi powder, bhuna jeera powder and salt.
6. Stir for 8- 10 minutes, stirring only occasionally. Too frequent stirring does not let the potatoes turn crisp. Keep the potatoes spread out while cooking. Check salt. Remove from fire.
7. Serve sprinkled with lemon juice and chopped coriander leaves.

Dal Makhani

Picture on page 4   *Serves 4-5*

1 cup urad saboot (whole black beans)
2 tbsp desi ghee
1½ tsp salt, 5 cups of water
1 cup ready made tomato puree
¼ tsp jaiphal powder, ½ tsp garam masala
1½ tbsp kasoori methi (dry fenugreek leaves)
2-3 tbsp butter, preferably white

GRIND TO A PASTE
2 dry, whole red chillies, preferably Kashmiri red chillies - deseeded & soaked for
10 minutes and then drained
1" piece ginger, 6-8 flakes garlic

ADD LATER
½ cup milk mixed with ½ cup cream or well beaten malai

1. Wash the dal, and soak in warm water for atleast 2-3 hours.
2. Drain water. Wash several times in fresh water, rubbing well, till the water no longer remains black.
3. Pressure cook dal with 5 cups water, 2 tbsp ghee, salt and ginger-garlic-chilli paste. After the first whistle, keep on low flame for 30 minutes. Remove from fire.
4. After the pressure drops, mash the hot dal a little. Keep aside.

5. To the dal in the cooker, add tomato puree, kasoori methi, garam masala and jaiphal powder.
6. Add butter. Simmer on medium flame for 30 minutes, stirring dal occasionally. Remove from fire. Keep aside to cool till the time of serving.
7. At the time of serving, add milk mixed with cream to the dal. Keep dal on fire and bring to a boil on low heat, stirring constantly. Mix very well with a karchhi. Simmer for 2 minutes more, to get the right colour and smoothness. Remove from fire. Serve.

Note: Originally the dal was cooked by leaving it overnight on the burning coal angithis. The longer the dal simmered, the better it tasted.

Khoya Matar

Serves 4

2 cups green peas (matar)
2 pinches hing, 2 laung (cloves)
100 gm khoya - mashed roughly or crumbled
½" piece ginger - finely chopped, 1 green chilli - chopped
1 tsp dhania powder, ½ tsp garam masala, ½ tsp red chilli powder, 1 tsp salt
1 large tomato - finely chopped, 1 tbsp chopped coriander

1. Heat 2 tbsp oil or ghee in a kadhai. Add hing and laung. Wait for 30 seconds.
2. Add khoya and stir fry on low flame, for about 3-4 minutes, till khoya becomes reddish brown.
3. Add the ginger, green chillies, and all the masalas (spices). Stir for a minute.
4. Add peas. Stir for 1 minute. Add ½ cup water and 1 tsp salt. Bring to a boil. Cook for 5-7 minutes on low heat, till peas are done.
5. Add chopped tomato and coriander. Cook again for 7-8 minutes till almost dry.

Methi Tamatar ← make this

Fenugreek leaves   *Serves 3-4*

1 large bunch methi leaves (500-600 gm)
2 pinches of hing
½ tsp sarson (mustard seeds)
½ tsp jeera (cumin seeds), 1 large tomato - chopped
½ tsp red chilli powder, ½ tsp salt, or to taste, ½ tsp dhania powder, ¼ tsp haldi

1. Pick methi leaves and chop coarsely. Wash in several changes of water. Keep aside.
2. Boil 8-10 cups water. Add methi to boiling water. Boil for 2-3 minutes. Remove from fire.
3. Strain methi leaves. Wash well under running water.
4. Squeeze out excess water and keep aside.
5. Heat 1 tbsp oil in a kadhai. Add hing, sarson and jeera. Wait for a minute till jeera turns golden.
6. Add chopped tomato and all the dry masalas. Stir for 2 minutes. Cook till oil separates.
7. Add 2-3 tbsp water and bring to a boil.
8. Add the squeezed methi leaves. Mix well. Cook on low heat for about 5-7 minutes on medium flame or till cooked. Serve hot with chappatis.

Sarson Ka Saag

Picture on page 76   *Serves 6*

1 bundle (1 kg) sarson (green mustard)
250 gm spinach (palak) or baathoo
2 shalgam (turnips) - peeled and chopped, optional
3-4 flakes garlic - finely chopped, optional
2" piece ginger - finely chopped
1 green chilli - chopped
¾ tsp salt, or to taste
2 tbsp makki ka atta (maize flour)
1½ tsp powdered gur (jaggery)

TADKA/TEMPERING
3 tbsp desi ghee
2 green chillies - finely chopped
1" piece ginger - finely chopped
½ tsp red chilli powder

1. Wash and clean mustard leaves. First remove the leaves and then peel the stems, starting from the lower end and chop them finely. (Peel stems the way you string green beans). The addition of stems to the saag makes it tastier but it is important to peel the stems from the lower ends. The upper tender portion may just be chopped. Chop the spinach or baathoo leaves and mix with sarson.
2. Put chopped greens with ½ cup water in a pan.
3. Chop garlic, ginger and green chilli very finely and add to the saag, add shalgam if you wish. Add salt and put it on fire and let it start heating.
4. The saag will start going down. Cover and let it cook on medium fire for 15-20 minutes. Remove from fire, cool.
5. Grind to a rough paste. Do not grind too much.
6. Add makki ka atta to the saag and cook for 15 minutes on low heat.
7. At serving time, heat desi ghee. Reduce heat and add ginger & green chillies. Cook till ginger changes colour. Remove from fire and add red chilli powder. Add ghee to the hot saag and mix lightly. Serve hot.
8. Serve with fresh home made butter and makki- ki-roti.

Note: When buying sarson, see that the saag has tender leaves and tender stems (gandal).

Bharwan Karela

Serves 4- 5

(300 gms) 6 karela (bitter gourd)
2 tsp salt, 3 tbsp vinegar
oil for deep frying, thread for tying the karelas

MASALA
1 tbsp saunf (fennel seeds) - powdered
1½ onions - finely chopped
½ of the scrapings (peel of the karelas)
½ tsp haldi, ½ tsp garam masala
2 tsp amchoor, 2 tsp dhania powder
½ tsp salt, ¼ tsp red chilli powder
¼ tsp sugar
1 tbsp achaar ka masala, preferably aam ke achaar ka masala

1. Scrape the karele. Preserve the scrappings (peel) for the filling. Mix half of the scrappings with 1 tsp salt. Keep aside. Throw away the rest of the peels (scrappings).

2. Slit the karela and remove the seeds.

3. Rub salt within and outside the karela liberally. Sprinkle 2 tbsp vinegar on the karelas and rub the karelas well.

4. Boil 5-6 cups water with 2 tsp salt. Put karelas in water and boil for 2 minutes. Remove from fire. Strain. Pick up the karelas and squeeze to remove bitterness. Wash again, squeeze and keep karelas aside. Wash scrapings well, squeezing well to remove the bitterness. Wash several times and squeeze well.

5. For masala, heat 3 tbsp oil in the kadhai, add onion, fry a little till it starts to turn golden. Add the washed and squeezed scrapping. Stir for 4-5 minutes till dry.

6. Add haldi, garam masala, amchoor, dhania powder, salt, red chilli powder sugar and aam ke achaar ka masala. Bhuno for another 5 minutes on low flame, stirring continuously.

7. Stuff the above mixture in the karelas and tie it with a thread to seal the filling.

8. Heat 1 cup oil for frying. Add the tied karelas and shallow fry for 5-7 minutes, turning sides till reddish brown on medium heat. Serve hot with paranthas and dal fry.

Sukhi Urad Dal

Serves 4

1 cup dhuli urad (split black beans) - soaked for 20 minutes
1 tbsp oil, ½ tsp jeera (cumin seeds), ½ tsp haldi, 1¼ tsp salt
¼ tsp garam masala, ¼ tsp dhania (coriander) powder, ¼ tsp red chilli powder

TEMPRING/TADKA
3 tbsp desi ghee/oil, a pinch of hing (asafoetida), ½ tsp jeera (cumin seeds)
1 onion - sliced very finely
¼ tsp red chilli powder, 1-2 whole, dry, red chillies - broken into 2 pieces
1 tsp shredded ginger or small thin strips of ginger (juliennes)

1. Strain the soaked dal and keep aside.
2. Heat 1 tbsp oil in a pressure cooker. Reduce heat, add jeera. Let it turn golden.
3. Add dal. Stir to mix. Add haldi, salt, garam masala, dhania powder and red chilli powder. Stir on low flame for 1 minute.
4. Add 1 cup water. Pressure cook to give one whistle. Keep on low flame for 1 minute only. Remove from fire immediately. Let the pressure drop by itself.
5. For the tadka, heat 3 tbsp oil in a small pan. Add hing and ¼ tsp jeera. Add onions & cook till they turn rich brown. Add chilli powder and whole red chillies. Immediately remove from fire and pour the tadka over the hot dal. Mix gently.
6. Serve hot garnished chopped coriander.

Mooli Tukdiyaan

serves 4

2 mooli (white raddish) - of medium thickness, 4 tbsp oil
1-2 tender leaves of mooli - shredded into thin long pieces

GRIND TOGETHER (ONION PASTE)
1 big onion, 2-3 flakes garlic, 1" piece ginger
2 tsp saunf (fennel seeds), 1 dry red chilli, ½ tsp sugar
2 tsp dhania powder, 1 tsp salt, ¾ tsp amchoor, ½ tsp haldi

1. Peel and cut each mooli into about 2-3" pieces. Slit each piece, like you slit a bhindi for saboot bhindi.Grind all ingredients of paste to a smooth paste.
2. Fill some paste in each piece. Rub left over patse over the mooli.
3. Heat oil in a kadhai. Add the mooli pieces and stir for 2 minutes. Cover and cook for about 20 minutes, stirring occassionaly till moolis turn soft. Serve hot.

Khoya Matar Makhaana

Puffed lotus seeds with peas in a rich gravy.

Serves 4

1 cup shelled peas (matar)
100 gms khoya (dried whole milk)
1¼ cup makhaanas (puffed lotus seeds)
1 tbsp khus khus (poppy seeds) - soak for 15 minutes in hot water & grind to a paste
3 tomatoes - pureed in a mixer
1 tsp dhania powder (coriander powder)
½ tsp red chilli powder, ½ tsp garam masala
salt to taste
1 tbsp kishmish (raisins)

GRIND TO A PASTE
2 big onions
1" piece ginger, 2 green chillies
1 tbsp chopped coriander

1. Fry makhaanas to a golden brown colour in oil.
2. Grind onions, ginger, chillies and coriander leaves with a little water in a mixer to a paste. Remove paste from the mixer.
3. Soak khus khus for 10-15 minutes & grind to a smooth paste.
4. Heat 4 tbsp oil. Add the onion-ginger paste. Cook on low heat till oil separates.
5. Add the khus khus paste. Cook for 1-2 minutes.
6. Add tomatoes pureed in a grinder. Cook till oil separates.

7. Add dhania powder, red chilli powder and garam masala.
8. Grate khoya. Add khoya and mix well for 1 minute.
9. Add peas. Mix well.
10. Add kishmish and salt.
11. Add enough water to get a thick gravy. Cook covered till peas are done.
12. Add makhanas. Give 1- 2 quick boils.
13. Serve hot, garnished with grated khoya.

Tip: Keep the khus khus in the fridge.

Jama Masjid ke
NON VEG SNACKS

Tips... (Do go through these to get perfect results)

- If your rolls or kebabs fall apart, quickly tear 1-2 slices of bread and grind in a mixer to get fresh bread crumbs. Add it to the mixture for binding.
- Never start frying in smoking hot oil as it will turn the snack black. Never fry in cold oil also as the snack may fall apart or it may soak a lot of oil.
- All boneless tikka recipes can be made with chicken with bones. Increase ¼ quantity of the marinade and all the other ingredients also, if using chicken with bones and grill for a little longer, for about 20 minutes atleast.
- For tikka, cut the pieces of food according to the space in between the wires of the grill. If the distance between the wires of the rack is too wide, and there is a chance of your piece slipping, then cover the wire rack with a well greased aluminium foil.
- The size of the tikkas should not be too small, because after getting cooked they shrink. A very small piece after getting cooked can turn hard after some time.
- While skewering or placing pieces of chicken, mutton, fish or even vegetable for grilling, the pieces should be arranged such that there is atleast 1" gap between them so that each piece can get its own space and heat all around to get cooked properly.
- Always place the tikkas or the kebabs on the grill or on the wire rack and never directly on a tray.
- Sometimes a little tandoori red colour or haldi added to the coating mixture or bread crumbs or maida gives a nice colour to the snack instead of the usual brown.
- For deep frying any snack, add small quantities to the oil at one time. This maintains the oil's temperature. If too many pieces are added together, the oil turns cold and a lot of oil is then absorbed by the snack.
- After deep frying, let the oil cool down. Add a little quantity of fresh oil to the used oil before reusing. This prevents the oil from discolouring.
- To check if the meat is cooked, pull with a fork. If it tears away, it is done.

Chicken Fry

Chicken pieces coated with spiced curd & fried.

Serves 4   *Picture on page 57*

500 gms chicken with bones - cut into 4 pieces and prick each piece with a fork on all the sides
1 cup curd - hang in a muslin cloth for ½ hour

PASTE (GRIND TOGETHER IN A MIXER)
1 onion, ½" piece ginger, 3-4 flakes of garlic
2 tbsp chopped fresh dhania (coriander)
1 tsp tandoori masala (optional)
a pinch of jaiphal (nutmeg) and javitri (mace)
seeds of 2 chhoti illaichi (green cardamoms), 1" stick dalchini, 1 tsp saunf (fennel)
2 saboot kali mirch (peppercorns), 2 laung (cloves)
1 tsp jeera (cumin seeds), 2 tsp saboot dhania (coriander seeds)
1 tsp salt, ½ tsp red chilli powder
½ tsp ajwain (carom seeds), 1 tsp garam masala

TO SERVE - SALAD (MIX EVERYTHING TOGETHER)
2 small capsicums - cut into ¼" small pieces, 2 onions - cut into rings
¼ tsp each of salt, red chilli powder, pepper
juice of 1 lemon, 1 tbsp poodina chutney

1. Hang curd in a muslin cloth for ½ hour.
2. Grind together all the ingredients written under paste to a smooth paste in a mixer. Use a little water if required. Remove the paste to a flat bowl.
3. Add hung curd and mix well.
4. Add chicken and keep aside in the refrigerator for atleast 4-5 hours or overnight.
5. Mix all the ingredients written under salad in a bowl. Keep salad in the refrigerator till serving time.
6. Heat oil in a kadhai, reduce heat to a low flame and fry 2 pieces at a time till golden brown. Let chicken pieces be in oil on slow fire so that the chicken gets cooked from inside. Remove from oil when chicken is properly cooked. Repeat with the remaining pieces.

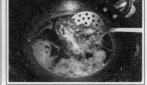

7. Sprinkle some lime juice on fried chicken and serve chicken with salad.

Gilafi Kebab

Picture on facing page   *Serves 8*

600 gm mutton mince (keema)
1 small capsicum - very finely chopped
1 tomato - remove plup and chop very finely
1 onion - very finely chopped, 4 green chillies - chopped
¼" piece of ginger - chopped, 2 tbsp ginger-garlic paste
2 tbsp lemon juice, 1 tsp garam masala, 2 tsp salt or to taste
¼ cup coriander - finely chopped

GRIND TO A PASTE WITH 1 TBSP WATER
1" stick of dalchini (cinnamon), ¼ tsp nutmeg, 4 cloves (laung), 4 tbsp kaju

1. Wash mince in a strainer (channi). Churn the mince 2- 3 times in a mixer to get smooth mince.

2. Mix together the mutton mince, chopped onions, green chilles, ginger, ginger-garlic paste, lemon juice, salt, coriander, freshly powdered whole spices, chopped tomato and capsicum. Mix well. Keep the mixture in the freezer for 1 hour.

3. Divide the mixture into 16 balls.

4. Make small kebabs with wet hands. Keep in fridge for 1 hour or more.

5. At serving time, heat 4 tbsp oil in a pan, fry 2- 3 kebabs on low heat till golden brown. Drain on napkins. Serve hot with hari chutney.

Note:

You can feeze these kebabs in freezer in a single layer in a plate. Cover plate with plastic wrap. Once frozen, you can place them, one on top of another in a box and use when required. They can be frozen for a week easily.

Use these kebabs in burgers to make delicious mutton burgers. Spread some mayonnaise on the bun halves, place the mutton kebab on it, top with onion rings and some shredded cabbage. Sprinkle a pinch of salt. Spread some mustard on the top half of the bun and place it on the other piece of bun. If you like insert a lettuce leaf also in between.

Chicken Fry : Recipe on page 55 ➢
Lahsun ki Chutney : Recipe on page 92 ➢

Special Chicken Pakoda

The chicken pieces are coated with curd & besan and fried to make them as soft as silk.

Serves 4

400 gms boneless chicken - cut into 2" pieces (8-10 pieces)
¾ cup milk

PASTE
seeds of 3 chhoti illaichi (green cardamoms)
¾" stick dalchini (cinnamon), ¾ tsp saunf (fennel)
2 saboot kali mirch (peppercorns), 2 laung (cloves)
1 tsp jeera (cumin seeds), 2 tsp saboot dhania (coriander seeds)
½" piece ginger, 2-3 flakes garlic, 1 tsp red chilli powder, ¾ tsp salt

COATING
7 tbsp besan (gramflour), 6 tbsp curd, 1 tbsp chopped fresh dhania (coriander)
½ tsp salt, ¼ tsp red chilli powder, ¼ tsp ajwain (carom seeds)

TO SERVE
2 capsicums - cut into 1" pieces, 2 onions - cut into 4 pieces
½ tsp garam masala, ¼ tsp salt

1. Grind together all the ingredients of paste in a small spice grinder to a smooth paste with a little water if required. Keep the ground masala paste aside.
2. Cut onion into 4 pieces and capsicum into 1" pieces.
3. Mix together ¾ cup milk with ¼ cup water in a kadhai. Heat and bring to a boil.

4. Add the above ground masala to the milk.
5. Add chicken also to the milk. Give 1-2 boils. Cover & lower heat. Cook for 8-10 minutes or till chicken is tender. Increase heat & cook till completely dry. Remove from fire. Cool.

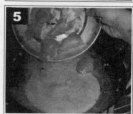

6. Place the cooked chicken in a bowl. Add all coating ingredients. Mix well.
7. Heat oil and fry few (2-3) pieces at a time on low heat till golden brown colour. Cook few pieces at a time, so that the chicken gets cooked from inside.

9. Mix pakodas with onion and capsicum. Sprinkle garam masala. Serve hot with tomato ketchup.

◄ Gobhi Samosa : Recipe on page 32

shami Kebab

Makes 15 kebabs

PRESSURE COOK TOGETHER
½ kg mutton mince (keema)
¼ cup channa dal - soaked in warm water for 20-30 minutes and drained
1 onion - sliced, 10 flakes garlic - chopped
2" piece ginger - chopped
2 tsp saboot dhania (coriander seeds)
1 tsp jeera (cumin seeds), 3-4 laung (clove)
2 chhoti illaichi (green cardamom), 2 moti illaichi (black cardamom)
½" stick dalchini (cinnamon), 1 tej patta (bay leaf)
4-5 saboot kali mirch (peppercorns)
2-3 dry, whole red chillies
salt to taste

1. Wash mince in a strainer and press well to drain out water. Add mince and all the remaining ingredients in a pressure cooker. Pressure cook to give 2 whistles. Keep on low flame for 2 minutes. Remove from fire.

2. When the pressure drops, uncover the pressure cooker. If there is any water left, keep the cooker on fire to dry the water. (If the mince is wet, the kebabs will break while frying). Do not cover the cooker.

3. When the mince turns dry, remove from fire. Let the mince (keema) cool down to room temperature. Grind the well dried mince in a mixer till smooth. Remove moti illachi.

4. Make balls. Flatten them to get thick, round 2½" diameter tikkis.

5. Roll the tikki on a flat surface to get neat edges and turn them into kebabs.

6. Shallow fry in a 2 tbsp oil in a pan on medium heat, till brown. Serve hot with poodina chutney.

Tandoori Chicken

Serves 6

1 medium sized chicken (800 gm) - cut into 4 pieces
1½ tbsp lemon juice of 1 small lemon
1 tsp red chilli powder, salt to taste
1 cup thick curd - hang in a muslin cloth for ½ hour
¼ cup thick cream
1 tbsp garlic paste
1 tbsp ginger paste
few drops orange red colour
½ tsp kala namak (black salt), 1 tsp garam masala
1 tbsp tandoori masala or chat masala
1 tbsp kasoori methi (dry fenugreek leaves)

1. Wash, pat dry chicken. Make incisions (deep cuts), 2 on the breast, 2 on the thighs and 2 on drumsticks.

2. Mix lemon juice, salt and red chilli powder. Rub on the chicken pieces and inside the incision. Keep aside for 2 hours in the fridge.

3. Mix curd, malai, garlic and ginger paste, kala namak, garam masala and colour together in a bowl. Rub the chicken all over with this mixture. Keep aside for 3-4 hours.

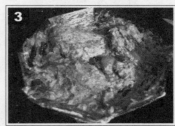

4. Heat the gas tandoor (flame should be minimum) or oven to 180°C. Place the chicken on the grill or wire rack (in the oven place a tray underneath the chicken to collect the drippings).

5. Grill for 10-12 minutes or till coating turns dry. Turn pieces and pour few drops of oil on each piece with a spoon. Grill for another 10-12 minutes, or till the chicken is dry and well cooked. Be careful not to make the chicken blackish and burnt.

6. Remove the chicken from oven. Sprinkle tandoori or chat masala and kasoori methi. Serve hot with onion rings and lemon wedges.

Chicken Tikka

Serves 4

2-3 breasts of chicken or 500 gm boneless chicken - cut into 2" pieces (8-12 pieces)

1st MARINADE
2 tbsp vinegar or lemon juice, ¼ tsp salt, ½ tsp chilli powder

2nd MARINADE
¾ cup curd - hang in a muslin cloth for 15-20 minutes
3 tbsp thick malai or cream
2 tsp ginger-garlic paste
½ tsp tandoori masala (optional)
¼ tsp black salt (kala namak)
½ tsp garam masala powder, ¼ tsp red chilli powder, ¾-1 tsp salt, or to taste
2-3 drops of red colour, 2 tsp oil
some chaat masala and lemon juice to sprinkle

BASTING (POURING ON THE TIKKAS)
2 tbsp melted butter

1. Wash the chicken pieces and pat dry on a kitchen towel.
2. Marinate the chicken pieces in the 1st marinade for ½ hour.
3. In a bowl mix all ingredients of 2nd marinade - curd, cream, ginger-garlic paste, tandoori masala, black salt, garam masala, red chill powder, salt, colour and oil.
4. Remove the chicken pieces from the 1st marinade. Add to the curd mixture and marinate for 6-8 hours in the refrigerator.
5. Heat an electric oven at 180°C or a gas tandoor on gas at moderate flame. Place the well coated the chicken pieces.
6. Roast for 15 minutes. Baste or pour some melted butter with the help of a spoon after 10 minutes on the chicken pieces or when the coating turns a little dry. Grill again for 5 minutes.
7. Sprinkle some chaat masala and lemon juice.

Note: The size of the tikkas should not be too small, because after getting cooked they shrink. A very small piece after getting cooked can turn hard after some time.

Kadhai Murg

A semi- dry preparation of chicken, flavoured with fenugreek and coriander.

Serves 4

1 medium sized (800 gms) chicken - cut into 12 pieces
6-7 tbsp oil
½ tsp methi daana (fenugreek seeds), 3 whole, dry red chillies
3 large onions - cut into slices
15-20 flakes garlic - crushed & chopped, 1 tbsp ginger paste
4 large tomatoes - chopped, ½ cup ready-made tomato puree
1½ tbsp saboot dhania (coriander seeds)
1 tsp red chilli powder, 1 tsp dhania powder (ground coriander)
2 tsp salt, or to taste, ¼ tsp amchoor, ½ tsp garam masala
½ cup chopped green coriander
1 capsicum - cut into thin long slices
2" piece ginger - cut into match sticks, 1-2 green chillies - cut into long slices
½ cup cream or ½ cup milk

1. Dry roast saboot dhania (coriander seeds) on a tawa lightly. Do not make them brown. Crush them on a chakla-belan (rolling board and pin) to split the seeds. Keep aside.

2. Heat oil in a kadhai. Reduce heat. Add methi daana and whole red chillies and stir for a few seconds.

3. Add onion and cook on medium heat till light brown.

4. Add garlic and stir for 1 minute.

5. Add chopped tomatoes. Cook for 4-5 minutes. Add ginger paste.

6. Add the saboot dhania, red chilli powder and dhania powder.

7. Add chicken and bhuno for 7-8 minutes on high flame, stirring well to mix everything together.

8. Add salt, amchoor and garam masala. Cover and cook for 10-15 minutes till tender, stirring occasionally.

9. Add tomato puree and chopped green coriander. Cook for 1-2 minutes.

10. Add the capsicum, ginger match sticks and green chilli slices. Mix well.

11. Reduce heat. Add cream or milk. Mix well for 2-3 minutes and remove from fire. Serve hot.

Nahari Gosht

Mutton cooked in an aromatic gravy with cardamom and finished with saffron and kewra.

Picture on page 75　　　　　　　　　*Serves 4*

½ kg mutton
5 tbsp ghee or oil
1 onion - chopped
1 onion - sliced
2 laung (clove), 1" stick cinnamon (dalchini)
2 bay leaves (tej patta)
seeds of 2 moti illaichi (black cardamom) - powdered
2 tsp coriander powder (dhaniya powder)
1 tsp red chilli powder , ½ tsp turmeric powder (haldi)
2½ tsp garlic paste (lasan) paste, 2" piece of ginger - crushed to a paste
salt to taste
1 cup dahi (yogurt)- well beaten
1 tsp maida (plain flour)
2 tsp gram flour (besan)
1 tsp garam masala
a few strands of saffron (kesar)
1 tbsp lemon juice
4 tbsp chopped green coriander
2-3 drops of tsp kewra essence or 2 tsp ruh kewra (optional)

CRUSH TOGETHER
seeds of 3 chhoti illaichi (green cardamoms)
¼ tsp mace (javitri), 1 tsp saunf (fennel seeds)

1. Powder all ingredients written under crush together in a small mixer grinder.
2. Heat the ghee in a pressure cooker, add the sliced onion, cinnamon sticks, and bay leaves, saute over medium heat until onion turn golden brown.
3. Add the mutton and bhuno for 10 minutes.
4. Add chopped onion, black cardamoms and cloves. Cook for 15 minutes.
5. Add the coriander powder, red chilli powder, haldi, garlic paste, ginger paste, and salt, saute until the oil separates.

6. Add the yoghurt and bring the mixture to a boil. Reduce heat to medium and cook for about 15 minutes. Give one whistle and cook for another 3- 4 minutes on low flame. Let the pressure drop by itself.

7. Add 2 cups water and bring to a boil again, cover and simmer for 10 minutes, stirring occasionally. Remove from fire.

8. Heat 1 tbsp ghee in a pan, add the maida and besan, saute over low heat, stirring constantly until light brown. Add the crushed spices, mix well. Remove from fire.

9. Add this mixture to the mutton and mix.

10. Add the garam masala, saffron and lemon juice; mix well and cook on low heat for 30 minutes. Remove from fire.

11. At the time of serving add kewra essence, mix well. Serve hot garnished with green coriander and with tandoori roti.

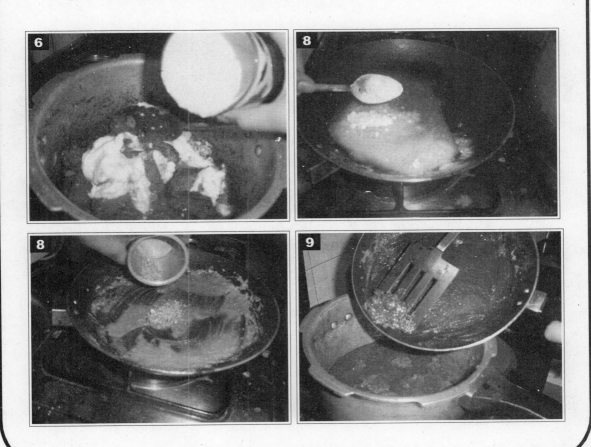

Murg Changezi

A classic culinary tribute to Gengis Khan, the Great Mongol.

Picture on page 3   *Serves 3- 4*

500 gms chicken with bones - cut into 6 pieces
3 onions - chopped
2 spring onions - chop the greens also

GRAVY
2½ tbsp ginger garlic paste
½ cup readymade tomato puree
1 tbsp black peppercorns - roasted on a tawa & crushed roughly
a pinch of jaiphal (nutmeg) - powdered (optional)
1 tsp salt, 1 cup milk
2 tbsp white or yellow butter
2 tbsp rum, ½ cup dahi (yogurt)
1¼ tsp haldi
1 cup water

1. Chop the white and green of spring onions separately.
2. Roast peppercorns on a tawa till fragrant. Crush roughly.
3. Heat 4 tbsp oil. Add and white part of spring onion. Cook till onion turns golden.
4. Add the chicken and stir fry for 8-10 minutes.
5. Add ½ cup curd and haldi. Mix well and cook for 2-3 minutes on low heat.
6. Add the tomato puree and cook for 5-6 minutes or till oil separates.
7. Add crushed pepper, garam masala, nutmeg and salt, simmer for 2 minutes,
8. Add 1 cup water, give 1-2 boils.
9. Add butter and milk, stir constantly.
10. Add greens of spring onion.
11. Remove from fire and add 2 tbsp of rum, stir. Adjust the seasoning. Serve hot.

Mutton Korma

Serves 6-8

1 kg mutton - cut into1½" pieces
4 onions - finely chopped or grated (2½ cups)
15-20 flakes of garlic
1 tsp haldi (turmeric) powder, salt to taste
1½ cups yogurt (dahi) - whipped with a fork
1 cup oil or ghee
1 cup cream (optional)
2-3 drops of tsp kewra essence or 2 tsp ruh kewra (optional)

CRUSH TOGETHER
2 small blades of javetri (mace), seeds of 6-8 chhoti illaichi (green cardamoms)
6 laung (cloves), ¼ tsp kesar (saffron)

GRIND TOGETHER
1½ tbsp saboot dhania (coriander seeds), 24 saboot kali mirch (peppercorns)
2" piece ginger, 1½ tsp red chili powder

1.   Grind garlic flakes with ½ cup water.
2.   Grind saboot dhania, ginger, kali mirch and red chilli powder to a paste in a small mixer. Keep aside.
3.   Crush javetri, seeds of chhoti illaichi, laung and kesar. Add ruh kewra or kewra essence.
4.   Heat oil/ghee, add grated or chopped onion. Cook till onions turn golden brown.

5.   Add garlic paste, cover the pan and cook for 5 minutes.
6.   Add mutton, haldi, salt and lightly beaten yogurt. Cover and cook till the liquid dries.
7.   Uncover the mutton. Bhuno mutton for 10 minutes or till golden brown.
8.   Add coriander seed-ginger paste. Mix well.
9.   Add 2 cups of hot water. Cover and cook on slow fire till the mutton becomes tender or pressure cook on high flame for 7 minutes and then reduce flame and cook for 5 minutes.
10. Add crushed ingredients and cream to the cooked mutton. Leave it over very slow fire for about 10-15 minutes.
11. Serve hot with steamed rice, chappati or nan.

Butter Chicken

An all time favourite! Tandoori chicken is prepared first and then this chicken is put in a rich, red gravy. The man behind the creation of butter chicken was Kundan Lal of Moti Mahal restaurant at Daryaganj.

Serves 4- 5

1 medium sized chicken (800 gm) - cut into 12 pieces
juice of 1 lemon
½ tsp red chilli powder, 1¼ tsp salt, or to taste

MARINADE
1 cup curd - hang for 30 minutes in a muslin cloth
2 tbsp thick malai or 2 tbsp cream
1 tbsp garlic paste or 8- 10- flakes of garlic - crushed to a paste
1 tsp ginger paste or ½" piece of ginger - crushed to a paste
1 tbsp kasoori methi (dry fenugreek leaves)
few drops of orange red colour
½ tsp kala namak (black salt)
1 tsp garam masala

MAKHANI GRAVY
2 tbsp butter, 2-3 tbsp oil, 1 tej patta (bay leaf)
2 tbsp ginger-garlic paste or 2" piece of ginger and 16- 18 flakes of garlic- crushed to a paste
½ kg (6-7) tomatoes - blanched, peeled and ground to a very smooth puree or 2 cups ready-made tomato puree
4 tbsp kaju (cashewnuts) - soaked in hot water for 15 minutes, drained and ground to a very fine paste with a little water
¼ tsp Kashmiri laal mirch powder or degi mirch
1 cup milk
2 tbsp cream
½ tsp garam masala
1 tsp tandoori masala
¼ tsp sugar or to taste

1. Wash, pat dry chicken. Make 2 incisions on breast, thighs and drumsticks.
2. Rub lemon juice, salt & chilli powder on the chicken and keep aside for ½ hour.
3. For the marinade, mix hung curd, malai, garlic and ginger paste, kasoori methi, kala namak, garam masala and colour. Rub the chicken with this mixture. Keep aside for 3-4 hours in the fridge.
4. Heat the gas tandoor (flame should be minimum) or oven to 180°C. Place the chicken on the grill or wire rack (in the oven place a tray covered with aluminium foil, underneath the chicken to collect the drippings). Grill for 15 minutes.

5. Brush pieces with oil or pour some oil with a spoon on all the pieces. Turn pieces and grill for another 10-15 minutes, till the chicken is dry and well cooked. Be careful not to make the chicken blackish and burnt. Keep tandoori chicken aside.

6. To prepare the makhani gravy, boil water in a pan. Add tomatoes to boiling water. Boil for 3-4 minutes. Remove from water and peel. Grind to a smooth puree. Keep aside.

7. Heat butter and oil together in a non stick pan or a kadhai. Add tej patta. Stir for a few seconds. Add ginger and garlic paste, cook until liquid evaporates and the paste just changes colour.

8. Add pureed tomatoes or ready-made puree, degi mirch and sugar. Cook until the puree turns very dry and fat separates.

9. Add prepared kaju paste, stir for a few seconds on low heat till fat separates. Add about 1 cup of water to get the desired gravy. Bring to a boil, stirring constantly.

10. Add tandoori chicken and salt. Cover and simmer for 5-7 minutes till the gravy turns to a bright colour. Reduce heat. Add milk on very low heat and bring to a boil, stirring continuously. Keep stirring for 1-2 minutes on low heat till you get the desired thickness of the gravy.

11. Remove from fire and stir in cream, stirring continuously. Add garam masala and tandoori masala. Stir. Garnish with 1 tbsp of fresh cream, slit green chillies and coriander. Serve hot with nan.

FINAL RECIPE

Note: To prepare tandoori chicken for butter chicken, if you do not have a tandoor or an oven, simply marinate the chicken as given and cook in a non stick pan or kadhai in some butter instead of a tandoor. For this, heat 4 tbsp butter in a pan. Add chicken pieces along with the marinade. Stir fry on medium high flame till the chicken is brown and crisp. Lower heat, cover and cook for 10 minutes till chicken is tender. Put this prepared chicken in makhani gravy.

Chicken Curry

Serves 4- 5

1 medium size chicken with bones (800 gm) - cut into 12 pieces
½ cup thick curd - well beaten with a fork or wire whisk
1¼ tsp salt, or to taste
6-7 tbsp oil
1 tej patta (bay leaf), 2-3 laung (cloves)
1" stick dalchini (cinnamon)
2 moti illaichi (brown cardamoms)
3-4 large onions - ground to a paste
½ tsp red chilli powder
2 tsp dhania powder (coriander powder), ½ tsp haldi
1 tsp garam masala
1½" piece of ginger and 10- 12 flakes of garlic- ground to a paste
2 tomatoes - pureed in a mixer grinder
1 tsp tandoori masala (barbecue masala) or ½ tsp bhuna jeera
2 tbsp chopped coriander (hara dhania)

1. Wash chicken well. Wipe with a clean cloth.
2. Mix chicken with well beaten curd and salt. Keep aside for ½ hour at least.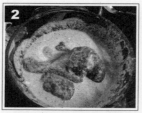
3. Heat oil in a heavy bottomed kadhai. Add 1 bay leaf, laung, dalchini and moti illaichi. Wait for a few seconds.
4. Add onion paste. Stir fry on medium heat till well browned
5. Reduce heat. Add red chilli powder, dhania powder, haldi and garam masala. Mix well.
6. Add ginger and garlic paste, stir for 1 minute.
7. Add the freshly pureed tomatoes. Cook for 5 minutes till oil separates and the tomatoes blend well with the onions.
8. Put the chicken pieces, leaving behind the marinade.
9. Bhuno well till the water evaporates and the chicken turns dry and glossy. (The chicken leaves its own fat).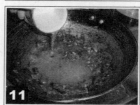
10. Reduce heat and add the marinade. Bhuno for 6-8 minutes more, till the curd dries completely & oil separates.
11. Add 2½ cups of water. Give 1- 2 boils. Cover and cook on low heat for 3-4 minutes till the chicken turns tender or pressure cook to give 1 whistle.
12. Add 1 tsp tandoori masala or ½ tsp buna jeera powder and mix well. Garnish with hara dhania.

Rogan Josh

The very popular Kashmiri mutton curry.

Serves 2-3

500 gms mutton - cut into small pieces
7 tbsp ghee/oil
3 laung (cloves)
1" dalchini (cinnamon)
2 moti illaichi (black cardamom)
2 tej patta (bay leaf)
½ tsp hing (asafoetida) dissolved in 1 tsp water
1½ tsp saunf (fennel) - powdered
½ tsp sonth (dry ginger powder)
1 tsp ginger paste
4 onions - ground to a paste
1 tsp ginger paste
1¾ tsp red chilli powder (degi mirch)
1½ tsp salt, or to taste, ½ tsp pepper powder
¾ cup curd (optional) - beat well till smooth
seeds of 7 chhoti illaichi (green cardamoms) - powdered
a little kesar (saffron) - dissolved in warm water

1. Heat ghee/oil in a cooker. Add laung, dalchini, moti illaichi and tej patta. Fry for 1- 2 minutes.
2. Add mutton and hing water. Fry for 15- 20 minutes till well fried. The mutton should become brownish in colour.
3. Add saunf, sonth, ginger paste, red chilli powder, salt and pepper. Fry for 3-4 minutes.
4. Reduce heat. Add powdered illaichi and curd. Keep stirring till it boils.
5. Add ½ cup water. Close the cooker and give 2 whistles. Keep on low heat for 10 minutes. (Mutton should become tender)
6. Open the cooker after the pressure drops. Add saffron. Simmer for 2-3 minutes and serve.

Murg Mussalam

Whole chicken in a rich almond gravy.

Serves 6

1 chicken (about 750 gm), you must buy a very small chicken broiler

MARINADE (GRIND TOGETHER)
1 cup yogurt (dahi)
10-12 flakes of garlic, 1" piece ginger, 2 green chillies
1" piece of raw papaya (kachha papita)
½ tsp red chilli powder
½ tsp garam masala, 1½ tsp salt, ½ tsp haldi (turmeric)

SPICES - ROAST TOGETHER FOR MASALA
1 tbsp saboot dhania (coriander seeds)
6 laung (cloves), 6 saboot kali mirch (peppercorns), ½ tsp jeera (cumin seeds)
1" piece dalchini (cinnamon)
seeds of 2 moti illaichi (brown cardamoms)
1 tbsp desiccated coconut (nariyal ka bura)
2 tbsp almonds - blanched (put in hot water for 15 minutes, peel skin and chopped)
a small blade of javitri (mace), a pinch of grated jaiphal (nutmeg)

OTHER INGREDIENTS FOR MASALA
6-8 tbsp oil
4 onions - chopped, 6 flakes garlic - chopped
1" piece ginger - roughly chopped
1 tsp salt, ½ tsp red chilli powder, ¼ tsp garam masala
1½ cups water
¼ tsp kesar (saffron) dissolved in 1 tbsp hot water
3 to 4 drops of kewra essence

GARNISH
1 tbsp chopped fresh coriander leaves
½ tsp kesar (saffron) soaked in 2 tbsp cream

1. Clean the chicken thoroughly and prick all over with a fork, make cuts over the breast and the legs if it is a little tough.
2. Grind the above-mentioned ingredients for the marinade into a fine paste.
3. Rub the ground paste into the chicken, all over the surface and the cavity. Leave chicken with this marinade for about 2 hours. Keep in the fridge.
4. To prepare the masala, lightly roast all spices in a clean kadhai given under spices, on low flame until fragrant. Do not make them brown. Remove from fire.

5. Heat 6-8 tbsp oil in a big kadhai (big enough to accommodate the whole chicken later). Add chopped onions and garlic. Do not add ginger. Remove onion and garlic from oil when they turn brown.

6. Grind all the roasted spices, browned onions and fresh ginger into a fine paste with a little water if required. Add salt, red chilli powder and garam masala to the paste. Keep the ground masala paste aside.

7. Heat left over oil, add ½ tsp red chilli powder. Stir and immediately add the marinated chicken and the left over marinade also. Cook for about 10-15 minutes till dahi dries up and the chicken turns brown.

8. After it is done, add the ground masala paste (prepared above, step 6) Add 1½ cups water. Cook chicken covered on medium heat till tender, about 40 minutes. Turn the chicken after 20 minutes. Sprinkle some hot water over the chicken if the water dries while cooking.

9. Mix the dissolved kesar in 1 tbsp hot water with the essence and sprinkle over the chicken when it is nearly cooked. Cook for about 5 minutes more or till a thick gravy remains and oil separates.

10. To serve, heat chicken. Transfer to an oval dish. Pour the kesar soaked in cream on the chicken. Sprinkle coriander & garam masala powder.

Final Recipe

Anda Parantha

Picture on facing page   Serves 4

DOUGH
2 cups atta (whole wheat flour), 2 tbsp oil
¾ tsp salt, ½ tsp red chilli powder
½ tsp ajwain (carom seeds), ½ tsp jeera powder (cumin powder)

OTHER INGREDIENTS
4 eggs
2 potatoes - boiled and mashed
salt to taste, ½ tsp red chilli powder, ½ tsp garam masala
oil or ghee for frying

1. Mix atta, oil, salt, red chilli powder, ajwain and jeera powder. Knead with enough water to a dough of rolling consistency. Cover and keep aside for 15 minutes.
2. Mix potatoes with salt, red chilli powder and garam masala.
3. Make 4 balls from the dough. Roll out a ball to a diameter of 5" like a poori.
4. Put a heaped tbsp of mashed potatoes (about ¼ of the mixture) in the centre. Collect the sides of the poori to cover the filling.
5. Flatten the stuffed ball slightly and press over dry flour. Roll out to a slightly thick parantha.
6. Carefully pick up the parantha and put it on a hot griddle (tawa). When the underside is cooked, turn to cook the other side. Smear some oil or ghee on the parantha. Trickle some oil on the sides too, around the edges. Turn the parantha to make it light golden.
7. When the parantha is almost done, shut off the fire. Make a 3-4" slit, a little away from the edge of the parantha. Open up the parantha from the slit with the help of a knife to get a pocket.
8. Break a whole egg in a small bowl. Put the egg all together in the pocket of the parantha. Return to low heat and let the egg in the parantha cook for 2-3 minutes on low heat. Remove parantha from tawa when it turns crisp and golden brown on both sides. Serve hot.

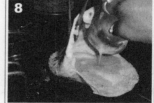

Nahari Gosht: Recipe on page 64 ➤

Varqi Parantha

Makes 8

Picture on page 2

2½ cups (250 gm) flour (maida), 1½ tsp salt
3-4 tbsp thick malai or thick cream, ½ tsp sugar, 2 drops of kewra essence
1 tbsp melted ghee

LAYERING
3 tbsp ghee, 3 tbsp maida

1. Sieve flour and salt in a mixing bowl or a parat.
2. Mix malai/cream and sugar in a small bowl. Add kewra essence and stir to mix.
3. Add the malai mixture to the maida and mix well. Knead with just enough water, adding about ¾ cup water gradually to make a firm smooth dough. Smear the prepared dough with some ghee to prevent it from drying, and cover well with a cloth napkin. Keep aside for 30-45 minutes.
4. Add 1 tbsp melted ghee to the dough. Mix well. Knead till smooth. Cover and again keep aside for 15 minutes.
5. Place dough on a lightly floured big surface like a kitchen platform. Roll out the dough into a big rectangular shape (like a tray) of about 12" long and 10" broad. Apply 1 tbsp ghee evenly over the rolled out dough, sprinkle 1 tbsp flour all over.
6. Fold about 4" (about 1/3) from top.
7. Fold the bottom over to get a strip with 3 folds.
8. Wrap strip of dough in a cloth napkin and keep in a plate. Put in the freezer of the refrigerator for 15 minutes. Take it out, roll it out again and fold in the same way as above and keep in the freezer wrapped in a cloth for another 15 minutes.
9. Remove from refrigerator, place on the floured surface, roll out again like a tray.
10. Cut small discs of 4" diameter with a round cutter or lid of any container.
11. Heat a tawa. Roll out the cut discs (parantha) to the thickness you like. Put on the hot tawa and cook both sides lightly. Pour some ghee on the sides and on top. Fry pressing sides with a paper tissue, till golden and cooked. Serve hot.

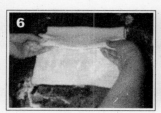
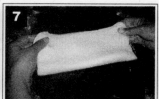

◄ *Sarson ka Saag : Recipe on page 50*
◄ *Makki ki Roti : Recipe on page 82*

Mashoor Gobhi/Paneer Paranthe

In the famous "Paranthe Waali Gali" in Chandani Chowk, I saw the paranthas being stuffed with the filling and then the filling being sprinkled with some dry flour. I wondered why the flour was being sprinkled on the filling and the next moment I guessed the reason. The flour absorbs any moisture present in the filling and thus makes the paranthas really crisp! Keep the paranthas a little thick with lots of filling inside.

Makes 8

FILLING
2½ cups grated cauliflower (1 big flower) or paneer
2 tbsp coriander - very finely chopped
1 tsp grated ginger
1 tsp amchoor, 1 tsp garam masala
1 tsp red chilli powder, 2 tsp salt

DOUGH
2 cups atta (whole wheat flour)
½ tsp salt
about ¾ cups water to knead

1. Prepare the dough by adding enough water to atta and salt. Cover and keep aside for 30 minutes.
2. Mix all ingredients of the filling lightly.
3. Take a big lemon sized ball of the dough. Roll it out to the size of a roti.
4. On the roti, put 3 tbsp of cauliflower, leaving 1" from all around. Sprinkle 1 tbsp of dry atta on it. Fold from all sides and make a ball again with the stuffing. Flatten ball and press on some dry flour to coat both sides.
5. Roll out to a round parantha. Keep the parantha thick, do not roll out too much.
6. Sprinkle a pinch of salt and red chilli powder on the parantha. Press with a belan (rolling pin).
7. Heat 2-3 tbsp ghee on a tawa. Shallow fry the parantha in ghee on the tawa till crisp on both sides. Trickle ghee from the sides while frying. Serve hot.

Katluma Parantha

A layered parantha.

Makes 10

3 cups maida (plain flour)
6 tbsp ghee plus ghee for frying
½ tsp salt
½ tsp red chilli powder
2 tbsp maida (plain flour)

1. Sift maida with salt. Gradually add enough water (about ¾ cup) to make a dough of rolling consistency. Cover dough with a cloth napkin. Keep aside for 30 min.
2. Melt 2 tbsp ghee and knead into the dough. Knead very well till the dough is soft and elastic.
3. To the remaining ghee mix 2 tbsp flour and make a paste of ghee and maida.
4. Make 10 balls. Roll out each to make a thick chappati.
5. Spread some ghee-maida paste all over.
6. Fold into half, again spread the ghee paste. Again fold into half to get a long strip.
7. Roll the strip like a pinwheel, to get a pedha (round flattened ball).
8. Keep the peda upright on the palm. Flatten it between the palms of the hands or gently roll on the chakla (rolling board) with the belan (rolling pin) without applying too much pressure, to a small thick parantha of about 6" diameter.
9. Put some ghee on the tawa. Heat ghee and put the parantha on the tawa. Trickle some ghee from the sides. Fry till rich brown on both sides on medium low heat. Press the sides and all over the parantha with a spoon while frying to ensure that it gets cooked since the parantha is a little thick.
10. Remove from tawa on to a clean kitchen napkin and press the hot parantha on the cloth from all sides for the layers to open up and turn flaky. Serve hot.

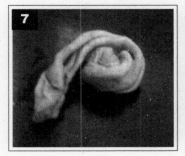 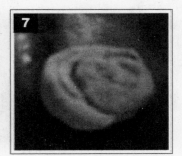

Bade Miya's Mutton Biryani

Makes 4-6

3 cups basmati rice
½ kg mutton - cut into 2" pieces
2 onions - sliced, 8-10 flakes garlic- chopped, 2" piece ginger- chopped
1 tej patta (bay leaf), 4 laung (cloves), 5 saboot kali mirch(peppercorns)
1" stick dalchini (cinnamon), 2 moti illachi (black cardamoms)
8 chhoti illaichi (green cardamoms)
1 tsp red chilli powder, 3 tsp salt
1 tsp dhania powder, 1 tsp garam masla
8 tbsp ghee or oil
¼ tsp orange colour, ½ tsp yellow colour, 2 tsp ruh kewra water (flavouring)

COARSELY POWDER TOGETHER & TIE SPICES IN A MUSLIN CLOTH
2 tsp saunf (aniseeds)
2 tsp saboot dhania (coriander seeds)
2 tsp jeera (cumin seeds)

1. Wash rice and soak for 20 minutes.
2. Put mutton in a pressure cooker. Add 1 tsp salt, muslin spice bag, garlic, ginger, tej patta, laung, chhoti illaichi, moti illaichi and 6½ cups of water. Pressure cook on high heat for 7-8 minutes and then on low heat for 5 minutes. Remove from fire and let the pressure drop by itself. Check that the mutton is tender. Put the mutton in a strainer and strain. Keep the liquid stock aside.
3. Heat ghee/oil in a kadhai. Add onion slices and fry till golden brown.
4. Add boiled mutton pieces, red chilli powder, dhania powder, garam masala and salt. Bhuno for 5 minutes.
5. Add the rice. Stir gently for 1-2 minutes.
6. Add 6 cups of stock of the boiled mutton. If less than 6 cups water , add some water to make it to 6 cups. Bring to a boil and cook it on low heat till the water gets absorbed and each grain of rice is separate.
7. Sprinkle orange colour on one half of the rice and yellow on the other half of rice. Do not mix.
8. On top of the colours sprinkle kewra water and keep it covered on very low heat for about 5 minutes. Serve after about 15 minutes.

Nan Badaami

Makes 6

2½ cups (250 gm) maida (plain flour)
½ cup hot milk
1 tsp baking powder, ½ cup warm water (approx.)
½ tsp salt
10 badaam (almonds) - cut into long thin pieces (slivered)

1. Heat milk and put it in a big bowl. Add baking powder to the hot milk. Mix well and keep it aside for 1-2 minutes.
2. Sift maida & salt together. Add maida to the hot milk. Mix.
3. Knead to a dough with enough warm water.
4. Keep in a warm place for 3-4 hours.
5. Make 6-8 balls.
6. Roll out each ball to an oblong shape. Spread ghee all over.
7. Sprinkle some chopped almonds. Press with a rolling pin (belan). Pull one side of the nan to give it a pointed end like the shape of the nan.
8. Apply some water on the back side of the nan. Stick in a hot tandoor.
9. Cook till nan is ready. Spread butter on the ready nan and serve hot.

Masala Paneer Nan

100 gm paneer
1 onion - chopped
½ tsp salt, ½tsp garm masala, ½ tsp red chilli powder
2 green chillies - chopped
2 tbsp coriander - chopped

1. Mix all ingredients together.
2. Make a dough as given above for nan badaami and keep in a warm place for 3-4 hours.
3. Make balls from the dough. Roll out the ball. Put 1 heaped tbsp of this filling in the centre of each nan. Pick up the sides to cover the dough.
4. Pat the stuffed ball on dry flour and roll to an oblong shape. Continue from step 7 onwards as given above.

Paneer Waale Bhatura

Serves 4

2 cups (250 gms) maida (plain flour)
1 cup (100 gms) suji (semolina)
½ tsp soda-bi-carb (mitha soda)
½ tsp salt, 1 tsp sugar
½ cup curd, preferably 1 day old
oil for deep frying

FILLING
75 gms paneer - mashed
½ tsp salt, ¾ tsp red chilli powder, ½ tsp garam masala

1. Soak suji in water, which is just enough to cover it.
2. Sift salt, soda and maida. Add sugar, curd and the soaked suji. Knead with enough warm water to make a dough of rolling consistency.
3. Knead again with greased hands till the dough is smooth.
4. Brush the dough with oil.
5. Keep the dough in a greased polythene and keep it in a warm place for 3-4 hours.
6. Make 8-10 balls. Roll out, put 1 tbsp of filling. Cover the filling with the dough to form a ball again.
7. Roll each ball to an oblong shape, and deep fry in hot oil till crisp and light golden.

Makki ki Roti

Picture on page 76   *Serves 4*

2 cups makai ka atta (maize flour)
hot water - to knead, ghee or oil for frying

1. Sieve the flour. Knead gently with hot water to a soft dough. Do not knead the dough too much in advance.
2. Tear an old polythene bag into two halves. Keep one piece on the chakla (rolling board). Put one ball of the kneaded dough on the polythene. Cover with the other piece, such that there is a plastic cover above and beneath the ball.
3. Now roll carefully with a rolling pin (belan) to a slightly thick roti.
4. Cook the roti on both sides on a griddle. Put some ghee and fry on low flame.

Missi Roti

Serves 4

1 cup besan (gram flour)
1 cup atta (whole wheat flour)
2 tbsp oil or melted ghee
1 tbsp kasoori methi (dry fenugreek lea
½ tsp salt, ½ tsp red chilli powder
½ tsp jeera (cumin seeds), a pinch of hing (asafoetida)
a pinch of haldi (turmeric powder)

1. Mix all ingredients. Add enough water to make a dough of rolling consistency.
2. Cover it and keep aside for ½ hour.
3. Make 6 balls.
4. Roll each ball into a chapati, but thicker than the usual chapati.
5. Cook on a hot tawa by frying it or in a hot tandoor.
6. When made in a tandoor, apply ghee and serve immediately.

Roomali Roti

Serves

DOUGH
1½ cups maida (plain flour), 1 cup atta (whole wheat flour)
2 tbsp oil, salt

PASTE
1 tbsp ghee, ½ tbsp maida (plain flour)

1. Make a dough with maida, atta, oil and salt. Keep aside for 1 hour.
2. Make a paste of the ghee and maida.
3. Make very small (lemon sized) balls of the dough.
4. Roll out balls of the size of a poori, then apply a tsp of the ghee-maida paste on of it. Cover it like a sandwich with the other poori and now roll out with a rolling pin (belan) to make a thin sandwiched roti.
5. Heat a tawa and cook this roti on both sides very quickly. Do not make it brown.
6. Remove from fire and immediately separate the 2 rotis stuck by the paste. Fold each roti like a hankey (roomal).

Daryaganj ka Rabri Falooda

Serves 4

2 cups falooda or rice seviyan - broken into short lengths, 1" pieces
4 cups rabri - chilled, recipe given below
2 cups crushed ice
½ cup rose syrup

1. Boil the falooda or seviyan in water for about 5 minutes until soft. Drain and refresh in cold water. Keep covered in the refrigerator till serving time.
2. To serve, take a tall glass. Put ½ cup rabri. Top with ½ cup crushed ice. Pour 2 tbsp of rose syrup on the ice.
3. Finish with ½ cup falooda. Stir gently to mix lightly. Serve.

Rabri

4 cups full cream milk
75 gm khoya - grated, (½ cup)
2 tbsp sugar
6-8 pistas - chopped
3 chhoti illaichi (green cardamoms) - powdered
rose petals or silver sheet (varq)

1. Boil milk in a heavy bottomed kadhai. Add khoya and sugar.
2. Simmer on low-medium heat for about 40-45 minutes, scraping the sides, till the quantity is reduced to almost half and the mixture turns thick with a thick pouring consistency. Remove from fire. The rabri turns thick on keeping.
3. Add some chopped pistas and cardamom powder into the mixture.
4. Transfer to a serving dish and garnish with pistas and rose petals.
5. Chill and serve plain by itself or with jalebis or with some fruit.

Daribe ki Jalebi

Serves 8   *Picture on page 93*

JALEBI
1 cup maida, 1 tbsp besan, ¼ tsp (level) soda-bi-carb (mitha soda)
½ tbsp melted ghee, ½ cup thick curd
3/4 cup warm water, ghee for frying

SYRUP
1¼ cups sugar, ¾ cup water, 2-3 pinches orange-red colour

1. Sieve maida, besan and soda. Add curd and melted ghee. Add enough warm water (about ¾ cup) to make a batter of a soft dropping consistency.
2. Beat batter well till smooth. Cover and keep aside for 30-40 minutes.
3. Heat ghee in a frying pan till medium hot. Put the batter in a piping bag and make circles within circle, starting from the outside.
4. Reduce heat. Fry them golden brown on low heat on both sides, turning carefully with a pair of tongs (chimta). Remove from oil, drain excess oil and keep aside.
5. For the syrup, boil sugar, water and colour in a kadhai. After the first boil keep on low flame for 5-7 minutes till a stringy syrup is attained.
6. At serving time, dip 4-5 jalebis at a time in the hot syrup for 1 minute, take out and serve them hot with rabri.

Kale Angoor ki Baraf

It is somewhat like a chuski. Enjoy it after a spicy chaat session.

Makes 6   *Picture on page 40*

2 cups black grapes (kale angoor)
2 tbsp powdered sugar, or to taste, ½ tsp lemon juice
½ tsp chaat masala, ½ tsp kala namak (black salt)

OTHER INGREDIENTS
6 large kulfi moulds, khus syrup, optional
6 wooden ice cream spoons or wooden satay sticks (long toothpicks)
aluminium foil

1. Put all ingredients with grapes in a mixer grinder and grind to a smooth puree.
2. Fill each mould only half.
3. Cover the top with aluminium foil. Insert a stick in the foil and place it in the freezer, keeping it upright. Freeze for 3-4 hours or till set.
4. Serve in a small glass, topped with a teaspoon of khus syrup.

Moong Dal Halwa

Picture on page 93   *Serves 8*

1 cup dhuli moong dal (skinned green beans)
10-12 chhoti illaichi (green cardamoms)
1 cup ghee, 2 tsp besan
1 cup sugar
1 cup milk
10-15 almonds - sliced, 10-15 kishmish (raisins)

1. Soak dal in water overnight or for 8-10 hours. Drain and grind to a fine paste in 2 batches (½ quantity at a time.)
2. Peel cardamoms and powder the seeds and keep aside.
3. Put the skin into a pan with the sugar and add 2 cups water. Stir over medium heat till sugar is dissolved. Simmer for 2 minutes on low heat. Remove from fire and keep aside.
4. Melt ghee in kadhai and fry the besan till lightly brown.
5. Remove from heat and add the dal paste. (This prevents dal from sticking to the bottom of the kadhai).

6. Reduce to medium heat and cook stirring, for about 25-30 minutes till golden brown.
7. Add milk a little at a time, stir for about 10-12 minutes, till ghee separates.
8. Stir and cook till golden. When done the fat will begin to separate.
9. Add the almonds and kishmish and cook for 2 minutes.
10. Strain the sugar syrup, add to the mixture and continue to cook and stir till water is absorbed. Bhuno the halwa for about 10 minutes till dry.
11. Sprinkle 2-3 tbsp ghee and cardamom powder. Bhuno on very low heat for 15 minutes till ghee separates and it turns to a rich golden yellow colour. Do not bhuno too much and let it turn brownish and overdone. Serve hot.

Kulfi

The real malaidar kulfi. Simply divine! Tha addition of just 1-2 drops of kewra essence makes all the difference. But add only a drop or two of the essence.

Serves 6

1 kg (5 cups) full cream milk
¼ cup sugar, or to taste
2 tbsp cornflour
75 gm fresh khoya - grated and mashed (¾ cup)
½ tbsp very finely cut almonds, ½ tbsp pistas - finely sliced
2 drops of kewra essence
seeds of 3-4 chhoti illaichi (green cardamoms)

1. Dissolve cornflour in 1 cup milk and keep aside.
2. Boil the rest of the milk in a kadhai or deep pan till it is reduced to half the quantity, for about 20 minutes on medium fire.
3. Add sugar and cornflour paste. Cook for 2-3 minutes more till sugar gets dissolved. Remove from fire. Let it cool down a bit.
4. Add khoya, almonds, pista, kewra essence and crushed illaichi.
5. Fill the mixture in kulfi moulds. Freeze for 6-8 hours or overnight.

Mango Kulfi

Makes 8

1 large mango chopped (1½ cups)
6½ cups full cream milk
7 tbsp sugar
seeds of 3-4 chhoti illaichi (green cardamom) - crushed
2 tbsp cornflour mixed with ½ cup milk
8-10 pistas - blanched & chopped
½ cup fresh cream

1. Keeping ½ cup chopped mango aside, puree the rest of the mango (1 cup) with ½ cup milk in a mixer.
2. Boil 6 cups milk with sugar and illaichi for about 20 minutes on low heat till it is reduced to about ½ quantity, about 3 cups.
3. Add cornflour paste stirring continuously. Stir for 5 minutes on low heat. Remove from fire and let the milk cool.
4. Add mango puree to thickened milk. Mix well. Add finely chopped mango pieces and finely chopped pistas also.
5. Add cream. Mix well. Pour into kulfi moulds and freeze for 5-6 hours or overnight.

Badaam ki Lauz

A very special Delhi sweet, which is niether a barfi nor a toffee, but something in between.

Makes 16 pieces

250 gms badaam giri (almonds without hard shell), about 1½ cups
½ cup sugar, ¼ cup water
varaq (silver leaf)

1. Put almonds in a bowl. Cover with boiling water. Leave for 15 minutes. Drain and remove skin. Grind blanched almonds coarsely.
2. In a heavy bottom kadhai, put sugar. Pour water on it and stir over low heat till sugar dissolves. Simmer on low heat for 2 minutes.
3. Add almonds and cook stirring continuously for 4-5 minutes, till mixture leaves the sides of the pan.
4. Transfer to a greased thali and level it with greased hands. Decorate with varaq. When cool, cut into squares.

Kheer

Rice is cooked in milk on low heat till it turns really creamy. Use a heavy bottomed kadhai to make the kheer and keep scraping the milk from the sides from time to time. Sugar is added after removing from fire. I still remember our cook "Moti" for his delicious kheer.

6 cups milk, preferably full cream
¼ cup uncooked rice - wash and soak for ½ hour
¼ cup sugar
seeds of 3-4 chhoti illaichi (green cardamoms) - crushed to a powder
a few almonds - sliced thinly

1. Boil milk in a heavy bottomed kadhai. Drain rice and add to the boiling milk. Cook on low medium heat for 30 minutes, stirring frequently and mashing the rice grains. Keep scraping the milk on the sides too. Remove from fire.
2. Add sugar and illaichi powder to the hot milk. Mix well till sugar dissolves.
3. Transfer to a servng dish. Garnish with almonds. Serve hot or cold.

Reheating Kheer ...

I had a very bad experience once with kheer. I was in a hurry to serve the kheer, so I put it on fire while I was doing something else also in the kitchen. I could not attend to it fully. It got burnt! The smoky flavour put off every one. The kheer should be reheated on very low heat and stirred constantly. Unattended kheer can be a disaster!

Kaju Fruit Rabri

A wonderful dessert. Serve it in individual mitti ke kasoore (earthernware bowls) to get the authentic flavour.

Serves 8

1 litre full cream milk
¼ cup cashewnuts - powdered coarsely
a pinch of mitha soda (soda bi carb)
1 tsp lemon juice
¼ cup sugar, or to taste
seeds of 5-6 chhoti illaichi (green cardamoms) - crushed

FRUITS
¼ cup green grapes - cut into half
¼ cup black grapes - cut into half
5-6 orange segments of a small orange - cut into half
¼ cup anaar
or
finely chopped apple with the peel (sprinkle apple pieces with 1 tbsp powdered sugar and a few drops lemon juice to prevent them from turning black)

1. Boil the milk in a heavy bottomed kadhai. Add powdered cashews and cook on medium low heat, for about 20-25 minutes, till it is reduced to about half the quantity.
2. Add soda, sugar and cardamom powder. Cook for another 5 minutes. Remove from fire and transfer to a mixing bowl. Scrape the sides of the kadhai also. Let it cool down.
3. Add lemon juice to the cold rabri and beat with a beater.
4. Transfer to individual serving bowls. Keep in the fridge for 15 minutes till the top layer sets a little.
5. Arrange fruits on the top of the rabri. Refrigerate till the time of serving.

CHUTNEYS

Hari Chutney

Serves 6

½ cup poodina leaves (½ bunch)
1 cup hara dhania (coriander) - chopped along with the stem
2 green chillies - chopped
2-3 flakes garlic - chopped finely
1 onion - chopped
1 tbsp lemon juice, or to taste
1½ tsp sugar, ½ tsp salt, a pinch of black salt (kala namak)

1. Wash coriander and mint leaves.
2. Grind all ingredients with just enough water to get the right chutney consistency.

Saunth (mithi imli chutney)

Serves 6

½ cup seedless imli (tamarind), 2 cups water
¾ cup gur (jaggery) powder or sugar, to taste
¼ tsp red chilli powder, ½ tsp saunf powder, ½ tsp dry ginger powder (sonth)
½ tsp jeera powder (cumin powder)
¼ tsp garam masala, ¼ tsp kalanamak or to taste

1. Wash imli 2-3 times. Soak imli in 2 cups of water for 10 minutes.
2. Add red chilli powder and bring to a boil, simmer for 2 minutes. Remove from fire and strain. Mash well to extract all the juice.
3. Add all the other ingredients and mix well. Boil. Simmer for 5-7 minutes till thick. Remove from fire and cool. Store in a bottle in the refrigerator.

Lahsun ki Chutney

Picture on page 57   Serves 8

15 flakes garlic - finely chopped
4-5 dry red chillies
1 tsp saboot dhania, 1 tsp jeera, 1 tbsp oil
½ tsp salt, 1 tsp sugar
2 tbsp lemon juice, or to taste

1. Break the stem of the red chillies and break into small pieces. Remove the seeds by tapping the chillies. Soak in 4- 5 tbsp hot water for ½ hour.
2. For the chutney, grind the soaked chillies along with the water, garlic, dhania, jeera, oil and sugar and lemon juice to a semi- smooth paste. Drain.
3. Heat 1 tbsp oil and cook for 2 minutes on low heat or till oil separates. Add ¼ cup water and bring to a boil. Simmer for 2 minutes. Remove from fire.

Dahi Poodina Chutney

Serves 6

GRIND TOGETHER
½ cup poodina (mint), ½ cup hara dhania (green coriander)
2 green chillies
½ onion, 2 flakes garlic

ADD LATER
1½ cups curd - hang for 15 minutes
a pinch of kala namak, ¼ tsp bhuna jeera, salt to taste
1 tsp oil

1. Hang curd in a muslin cloth for 15 minutes. Keep aside.
2. Wash coriander and mint leaves.
3. Grind coriander, mint, green chillies, onion and garlic with a little water to a paste.
4. Beat hung curd well till smooth.
5. To the hung curd, add the green paste, oil, kala namak, bhuna jeera and salt to taste.

Daribe ki Jalebi : Recipe on page 85 ➤
Moong Dal Halwa : Recipe on page 86 ➤

BEST SELLERS BY *Nita Mehta*

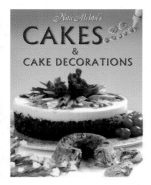

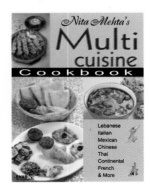

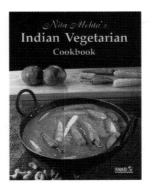

BEST SELLERS BY *Nita Mehta*

Nita Mehta's
101 CHICKEN Recipes

Nita Mehta's
BAKES & CAKES
Baking With Confidence!

Nita Mehta's
CHINESE
Cooking For The Indian Kitchen

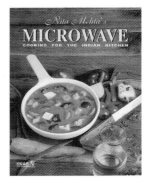
Nita Mehta's
MICROWAVE
COOKING FOR THE INDIAN KITCHEN

Nita Mehta's
Different ways with Paneer
Vegetarian

Nita Mehta's
VEGETARIAN
Mughlai

Nita Mehta's
VEGETARIAN
Chinese

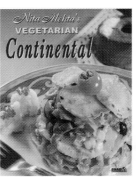
Nita Mehta's
VEGETARIAN
Continental

Nita Mehta's
The Best of
CHICKEN & PANEER

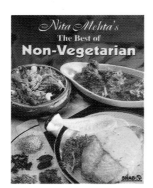
Nita Mehta's
The Best of
Non-Vegetarian

Nita Mehta's
Punjabi
Khaana

Nita Mehta's
Low Calorie
cooking for the Indian kitchen

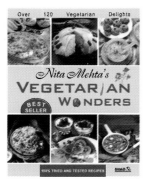
Over 120 Vegetarian Delights
Nita Mehta's
VEGETARIAN WONDERS
BEST SELLER
100% TRIED AND TESTED RECIPES

Nita Mehta's
VEGETARIAN
Snacks
100% TRIED & TESTED RECIPES

Nita Mehta's
CONTINENTAL
cooking for the Indian kitchen

Nita Mehta's
VEGETARIAN
Microwave
COOKBOOK
COOKING, BAKING AND GRILLING
100% TRIED & TESTED RECIPES

BEST SELLERS BY *Nita Mehta*

Nita Mehta's
VEGETARIAN
Punjabi

Nita Mehta's
GREAT
Indian
COOKING

Vegetarian

Nita Mehta's
ITALIAN
cooking for the Indian kitchen

100% TRIED AND TESTED RECIPES

Nita Mehta's
Simply Delicious
CURRIES

COOKING BAKING GRILLING
Nita Mehta's
Everyday
Microwave
Cooking

100% TRIED & TESTED RECIPES

Nita Mehta's
SUBZIYAAN
Tasty VEGETABLES for EVERYDAY cooking

Vegetarian

Nita Mehta's
TANDOORI
COOKING
in the OVEN

Nita Mehta's
TEMPTING
SNACKS

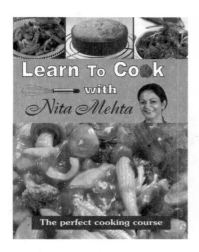

Learn To Cook
with
Nita Mehta

The perfect cooking course

Nita Mehta's
Flavours of
Indian Cooking

Award Winner

Nita Mehta's

OATS BREAKFAST COOKBOOK

A fresh approach to a healthier natural breakfast

LEARN TO COOK   Step by Step
CHOCOLATE
Nita Mehta

LEARN   Step by Step
Food Styling, Garnishing
& Table Laying
Nita Mehta

LEARN TO COOK   Step by Step
PIZZA & PASTA
Nita Mehta

Vegetarian

LEARN TO COOK   Step by Step
Lebanese
Nita Mehta

NITA MEHTA
COOKERY CLUB
Become a MEMBER

Get FREE Cookooks

www.nitamehta.com

CLICK HERE

Become a Member

Get Free Cookbooks

nita mehta.com
Recipes, Cook Books, Classes & Much more.

Book Search

About Nita Mehta
International Award Winner
Reviews & Comments
Order outside India

Cooking Tips
Self Help & Fitness
Recipe of the Week
Business Opportunities
Interactive Events

Cookery Books
Indian Cuisine
International Cuisine
Low Calorie Books
Microwave Cooking
Other Books
Hindi Books
Complete List of Books

Welcome !

Where to Buy | Ask Nita Mehta

What's New

Nita Mehta's
Cooking for
Growing
Children

Cookery Classes

Meet
the author
& enjoy
interactive
cookery
sessions

NITA MEHTA

Cook Books by Nita Mehta

Children Books

Members Area

Login

Password

login

• Register   • Forgot Password

Register at : www.nitamehta.com
Now you can buy Nita Mehta books with your credit card
Buy Online at www.nitamehta.com